HOW TO LOCATE GOVERNMENT EMPLOYMENT

INCLUDING INFORMATION ABOUT

**State
County
&
Local Jobs**

BY

ROBERT HANCOCK

and

ELIZABETH ASHTON

ISBN 0-934748-30-6

Manufactured in the United States of America

PUBLISHER'S NOTE

We have done our best to carefully research and compile this Directory only from sources believed to be authentic and reliable; however, we cannot guarantee total accuracy or completeness.

If you would be kind enough to bring to our attention any errors you may find, we will include your corrections in our next edition. We will also send you a complimentary copy of one of our other reports as a token of our appreciation.

Please note we are not affiliated with any Governmental Agency. Our sole purpose is to provide you with a fund of useful information.

Best of Luck.

THE PUBLISHERS

Acknowledgement

The material used in this Directory is drawn in part from government publications. Their contribution is gratefully acknowledged.

CONTENTS

1.0 FOREWORD

Thank you for purchasing this directory. We have tried very hard to gather an enormous amount of information into one publication for you. At your fingertips you have a very powerful tool to help you find the most important thing we all need -- A JOB! And not just any job, but one of THE most valuable jobs available -- a **Government Job** with all its security, benefits and impressive pay scales.

The most important thing now is to USE this information -- only if you do will it be worth many times the money you have paid for it. Remember, it is a **working** manual -- make notations in the pages as you go along and in the margin areas as you work with it.

Incidentally, the money you invested in this Directory is literally a small drop in the bucket compared to the enormous benefits you can realize from it. Remember, your time is valuable -- Government Jobs are always available (if you know where to look), and the sooner you get organized and start applying for the opportunities suited to you, the better.

We have spent many hours researching information, compiling and writing to bring you this directory which is going to help you to efficiently get the precise Government Job you've always wanted. It could well be worth a hundred times the price you paid. If you don't believe me, ask yourself just how much would you pay, right now, if some Government official walked in the door and offered you the job you wanted?

Somebody once said that if you want to milk a cow you do not sit on a stool in the middle of the field and wait for the cow to back up to you? So now it's your turn. You've been smart enough to invest in this directory -- now make it the best investment you've ever made.

And remember, don't let anyone tell you that you cannot find an excellent Government Job. You **can**. And when you do, it will likely open up a whole new life you never knew even existed.

Good luck in your job search.

2.0 INTRODUCTION

I don't care where you live, whether you are unskilled, untrained or an unemployed dropout. I don't care whether you completed 10th grade, are a new graduate or a seasoned professional... YOU CAN GET A WELL-PAYING AND SECURE GOVERNMENT JOB. There are literally hundreds of thousands of jobs available right now with pay scales ranging from $11,478 per year to in excess of $83,000 per year. You think of what sorts of jobs you'd like to do and the government has them. Period. Our government is far and away the largest employer in the land, providing jobs for over <u>16 MILLION</u> civilian workers -- about 1 out of 6 employed persons in the whole United States.

Of these 16 millions jobs, about <u>11 MILLION</u> persons work locally for their State and Local Governments (county, city, township, school district or other special divisions. The remainder, around <u>5 MILLION</u>, work for the Federal Government.

3.0 AN OVERVIEW OF GOVERNMENT EMPLOYMENT

The U.S. Government is the largest employer in the nation. With over 3 million people in their civilian work force, the government must hire several hundred people each and every day to replace those lost through attrition. Nearly 98 percent of the federal employees work in the Executive Branch of the government. The remainder work in the Legislative and Judicial Branches. You will find federal employees in jobs throughout the world. About 94 percent work in the U.S. with the remaining 6 percent filling positions overseas. While we consider Washington, D.C. the center of our government, only 14 percent of the government's work force is actually based there. Employment opportunities abound in the 50 states.

Our government is full of departments and agencies varying in size and function. The Department of Defense currently employs nearly half of the federal work force. Other large departments include Agriculture, Health and Human Services, Justice, Treasury and Veterans Affairs.

The smaller departments and agencies employ fewer workers, but there are still jobs to be found. Throughout this book we will be giving you detailed background information on the various agencies and types of work you can expect in each. As you read, you will have a much greater understanding of the diversity which exists among the various government entities so that you can determine where you best fit in.

3.1 FEDERAL PERSONNEL CLASSIFICATION SYSTEM

Federal employees labor in basically the same kinds of jobs which exist in the private sector. You'll find government architects -- and zoologists -- with about 900 other professions in between. There are a few jobs, such as customs inspectors or air traffic controllers, which exist only in the government. Jobs within the government tend more toward white collar and professional than jobs in the economy as a whole. In fact, nearly 80 percent of the federal employees hold white collar positions. Only one out of five employees are considered to hold blue collar positions. The trend toward white collar jobs within the government is on the upswing, and it is felt this trend will continue throughout this century.

The federal white collar personnel classification system includes an Occupational Group structure grouping like jobs together. There are 22 Occupational Groups ranging from GS-000 to GS 2100. Each Occupational Group has its own group number and title which keeps it distinct from every other Group. Here is a listing of the government's current groupings:

GS-000   Miscellaneous
GS-100   Social Science, Psychology and Welfare

GS-200	Personnel Management & Industrial
GS-300	Administrative, Clerical and Office Services
GS-400	Biological Sciences
GS-500	Accounting and Budget
GS-600	Medical, Hospital, Dental & Public Health
GS-700	Veterinary Medical Science
GS-800	Engineering and Architecture
GS-900	Legal and Kindred
GS-1000	Public Information and Arts
GS-1100	Business and Industry
GS-1200	Copyright, Patent and Trademark
GS-1300	Physical Sciences
GS-1400	Library and Archives
GS-1500	Mathematics and Statistics
GS-1600	Equipment, Facilities and Service
GS-1700	Education
GS-1800	Investigation
GS-1900	Quality Assurance, Inspection and Grading
GS-2000	Supply
GS-2100	Transportation

Each Occupational Group has an identifier which contains three parts: the Pay System, the Occupational Group Number and the Title. An example would be:

GS-200, Personnel Management and Industrial Relations - the GS means the job is in the General Schedule (or white collar) pay system. 200 is the Occupational Group Number, and Personnel Management and Industrial Relations is the Occupational Group Title. Every Occupational Group contains the individual jobs comprising the Group with their corresponding Job Series Numbers and Titles. Excluded from the Occupational Groups are approximately 100 of the smallest white collar occupations; all of the blue collar (wage grade) occupations, and most of the occupations in the Excepted Service.

3.2 A CLOSER LOOK AT THE GS GROUPINGS

When you are looking for government employment, the better you understand the system, the better your chances of landing a job. Let's take a closer look at what each of the Occupational Groups have to offer.

GS-000 Miscellaneous Occupations: What do park rangers, chaplains, correctional officers and guards have in common? All of these jobs are unrelated to any other Occupational Group so they have been placed in the Miscellaneous Group. This group includes all classes of positions which have responsibilities to administer, supervise or perform work not included in any other occupational group

6

either because the duties are unique, complex or come partially under a variety of other groups. Occupations found in this group include: bond sales promotion representatives (GS-011), chaplains (GS-060), community planners (GS-020), correctional institution administrators (GS-006), correctional officers (GS-007), environmental protection assistants (GS-029), environmental protection specialists (GS-028), fingerprint identifiers (GS-072), firefighters and fire inspectors (GS-081), outdoor recreation planners (GS-023), park rangers and park managers (GS-025), police officers (GS-083), safety and occupational health specialists (GS-018), safety technicians (GS-019), security guards (GS-085), security specialists (GS-080), sports specialists (GS-030),and U.S. Marshals (GS-082).

GS-100 SOCIAL SCIENCE, PSYCHOLOGY AND WELFARE: Social sciences and social services deal with cultures and people. Social sciences deal with psychology, history, anthropology, sociology, and economics. Social services deal with social work, recreational activities, and the administration of public welfare and insurance programs. The positions in this group carry responsibilities for advising, administering, supervising or performing research or other professional and scientific work, subordinated technical work or related clerical work. Occupations in this group include: anthropologists (GS-190), archaeologists (GS-193), economists (GS-110), foreign agricultural affairs specialists (GS-135), food assistance program specialists (GS-120), foreign affairs specialists (GS-130), geographers (GS-150), historians (GS-170), intelligence aids and clerks (GS-134), intelligence specialists (GS-132), manpower development specialists (GS-142), psychologists (GS-180), psychology aides and technicians (GS-181), recreation specialists (GS-188), social insurance administrators (GS-105), social science aides and technicians (GS-102), social scientists (GS-101), social service aides and assistants (GS-186), social service representatives (GS-187), social workers (GS-185), and unemployment insurance specialists (GS-106).

GS-200 PERSONNEL MANAGEMENT AND INDUSTRIAL RELATIONS: The force that makes the wheels of our government move is called manpower. Each agency has a personnel office staffed with personnel specialists who hire, fire, and train employees. Additionally they administer a variety of personnel programs and perform work involving the various aspects of human resources management and industrial relations. Occupations contained in this group include: apprenticeship and training representatives (GS-243), contractor industrial relations specialists (GS-246), employee development specialists (GS-235), employee relations specialists (GS-230), equal employment opportunity specialists (GS-260), labor management relations examiners (Gs-244), labor relations specialists (GS-233), mediators (GS-241), military personnel clerks and technicians (GS-204), military personnel management specialists (GS-205), personnel clerks and assistants (GS-203), personnel management specialists (GS-201), personnel staffing specialists (GS-212), position classification specialists (GS-221), salary and wage administrators (GS-223), and wage and hour compliance specialists (GS-249).

GS-300 ADMINISTRATIVE, CLERICAL AND OFFICE SERVICES: This grouping contains jobs which have responsibilities for administering, supervising or performing work involving management analysis, stenography, typing, and secretarial work. Also included are mail and filing tasks, the operations of computers, office machines, and communications equipment; as well as the technical phases of photographic and art processes. Occupations in this group include: administrative officers (GS-341), clerk-stenographers and reports (Gs-312), clerk-typists (GS-322), closed microphone reporters (GS-319), coding clerks (GS-357), communications clerks (GS-394), communications managers (GS-391), communication relay operators (GS-390), communications specialists (GS-393), computer clerks and assistants (GS-335), computer operators (GS-332), computer specialists (GS-334), correspondence clerks (GS-309), data transcribers (GS-356), equal opportunity compliance specialists (GS-360), equipment operators (GS-350), general communications specialists (GS-392), logistics management specialists (GS-346), mail and file clerks (GS-305), management analysis(GS-343), management clerks and assistants (Gs-344), miscellaneous clerks and assistants (GS-303), program analysts (GS-345), secretaries (GS-318), and support services administrators (GS-342). **It should be noted that a shortage exists in the federal government of qualified secretaries, clerks, typists and stenographers.**

GS-400 BIOLOGICAL SCIENCES: By studying what happens to cells, animals, plants, insects and soils the biologists and related scientists can use their knowledge to detect and control pests and diseases. They can also develop new strains and promote growth of useful organisms. This occupational grouping carries the responsibility for advising, administering, supervising or performing research or other professional and scientific or technical work in any of the science fields concerned with living organisms; the soil and its properties and distribution; and the management, conservation and use of these resources. Jobs in this group include: agricultural management specialists (GS-475), agronomists (Gs-471), animal scientists (GS-487), biological technicians (Gs-404), botanists (Gs-430), ecologists (GS-408), entomologists (GS-414), fish and wildlife administrators (GS-480), fish and wildlife refuge managers (GS-485), fishery biologists (GS-482), foresters (GS-460), forestry technicians (GS-462), general biological scientists (GS-401), geneticists (GS-440), home economists (GS-493), horticulturists (GS-437), irrigations system operators (GS-459), microbiologists (GS-403), pharmacologists (GS-405), physiologists (GS-413), plant pathologists (GS-434), plant physiologists (GS-435), plant protection and quarantine officers (GS-436), plant protection technicians (GS-421), range conservationists (GS-454), range technicians (GS-455), soil conservationists (GS-457), soil conservation technicians (GS-458), soil scientists (GS-470), wildlife biologists (GS-486) and zoologists (GS-410).

GS-500 ACCOUNTING AND BUDGET: When you're dealing with money on the level with which the federal government does -- someone has to be accountable. The federal government employs financial experts in virtually all of its agencies for just this reason. The people who hold these positions advise, administer, supervise or perform professional, technical or other related clerical work of an accounting, budget administration or financial management nature. The occupations in this group include: accountants (GS-510), accounting technicians (GS-525), auditors (GS-511), budget analysts (GS-560), cash processors (GS-530), financial administrators (GS-501), financial institution examiners (GS-570), financial managers (GS-505), insurance accounts specialists (GS-593), internal revenue agents (GS-512), military pay specialists (GS-545), payroll clerks and technicians (GS-544), tax examiners (GS-592), tax technicians (GS-526), and voucher examiners (GS-540).

GS-600 MEDICAL, HOSPITAL, DENTAL AND PUBLIC HEALTH: Our nation's health is regulated, maintained and perfected upon by the doctors, dentists, therapists, allied health specialists, nurses, health administrators and health care support staff working for the federal government. The individuals in these positions counsel, oversee, guide or implement research work in one of the many branches of medicine, surgery, dentistry and related patient care occupations. The occupations included in this group are: autopsy assistants (GS-625), consumer safety officers (GS-696), corrective therapists (GS-635), dental assistants (GS-681), dental hygienists (Gs-682), dental laboratory aides and technicians (GS-683), dentists (GS-680), diagnostic radiologic technologists (GS-647), dietitians and nutritionists (GS-630), doctors (GS-602), educational therapists (GS-639), environmental health technicians (GS-698), general health scientists (GS-601), health aides and techs (GS-640), health system administrators (GS-670), health system specialists (GS-671), hospital housekeepers (GS-673), industrial hygienists (Gs-690), manual arts therapists (GS-637), medical clerks (GS-679), medical machines techs (GS-649), medical records librarians (GS-669), medical records techs (GS-675), medical supply aides and techs (GS-622), medical techs (GS-644), nuclear medicine techs (GS-642), nurses (GS-610), nursing assistants (GS-621), occupational therapists (GS-631), optometrists (GS-662), orthotist/prosthetists (GS-667), pathology techs (GS-646), pharmacists (GS-660), pharmacy techs (GS-661), physical therapists (Gs-633), physicians assistants (GS-603), podiatrists (Gs-668), practical nurses (Gs-620), prosthetic reps (GS-672), public health advisors and analysts (GS-685), recreation and creative arts therapists (GS-638), rehabilitation therapy assistants (GS-636), respiratory therapists (GS-651), restoration techs (GS-664), speech pathologists and audiologists (GS-665), therapeutic and radiologic technologists (GS-648). Opportunities abound in the public sector for doctors and dentists, audiologists, dietitians, medical records administrators, orthotist/prostetists, pharmacists, speech pathologists, physical therapists and nurses across the U.S.

GS-700 VETERINARY MEDICAL SCIENCE: Livestock diseases, meat and poultry processing operations, laboratory research, and animal health and welfare are areas of concern to the federal government. Management and elimination of animal diseases is a primary objective. The positions in this group carry responsibilities for advising and consulting, administering, managing, supervising or performing research or other professional and scientific work in the various branches of veterinary medical science. The occupations in this group include: animal health techs (GS-704) and veterinarians (GS-701).

GS-800 ENGINEERING AND ARCHITECTURE: Engineers and architects perform professional and scientific work in the design and construction of projects such as buildings, systems, equipment and materials and methods. Additionally, they review applications, designs, and plans for structures and systems. To qualify for a position in this grouping you need a knowledge of the science or the art (or both) in order to transform and make useful materials, natural resources and power. The occupations in this group include: aerospace engineers (GS-861), agricultural engineers (GS-890), architects (GS-808), biomedical engineers (GS-858), chemical engineers (GS-893), civil engineers (Gs-810), construction analysts (GS-828), drafting engineers (GS-818), electrical engineers (GS-850), electronics engineers (GS-855), electronic techs (GS-856), engineering techs (GS-802), engineers (GS-801), environmental engineers (GS-819), fire prevention engineers (GS-804), industrial engineering techs (GS-895), industrial engineers (GS-896), materials engineers (GS-806), mechanical engineers (GS-830), mining engineers (GS-880), naval architects (GS-871), petroleum engineers (GS-881), safety engineers (GS-803), ship surveyors (GS-873) and surveying techs (GS-817). **There are numerous opportunities for engineers in all specialties with the federal government across the U.S.**

GS-900 LEGAL AND KINDRED: The drama of the courtroom, and our wonderful and complex laws demand the attention of lawyers, judges and examiners. Any agency is likely to employ attorneys either in its legal department or in its Office of the General Counsel. This group includes all sectors of work which carry responsibilities for advising, directing, overseeing or executing professional legal work in preparation for the trial and argument of cases; presiding at formal hearings; administering laws entrusted to an agency or department; providing undistorted or advisory legal opinions or decisions; preparing a variety of legal documents; and performing quasi-legal work. The occupations contained in this group include: administrative law judges (Gs-935), attorneys (GS-905), civil service retirement claims examiners (GS-997), claims clerks (GS-998), contact representatives (GS-962), general claims examiners (GS-990), hearings and appeals specialists (GS-930), land law examiners (GS-965), legal clerks and technicians (GS-986), loss and damage claims examiners (GS-992), paralegal specialists (GS-950), social insurance claims examiners (GS-993), unemployment compensation claims examiners (GS-994), veterans claims examiners (GS-996), visa and passport examiners (GS-967) and worker's compensation claims examiners (GS-991).

GS-1000 PUBLIC INFORMATION AND ARTS: You probably don't realize that there is a branch of government dealing with music, theater, language, etc. This is certainly not the typical federal job most people envision. And yet, the world of public information, museums, photography, writing and illustrating are all very much

10

a part of our government's work. The federal government operates and maintains theaters, audio-visual production facilities, museums, and public information programs. Individuals employed in this group are writers, editors, language and foreign language interpreters, technicians and clerks. The occupations in this group include: arts specialists (GS-1056), audio-visual production specialists (GS-1071), editorial assistants (GS-1087), exhibits specialists (GS-1010), illustrators (GS-1020), language specialists (GS-1040), museum curators (GS-1015), museum specialists and technicians (GS-1016), photographers (GS-1060), public affairs specialists (GS-1035), technical writers and editors (GS-1083), visual information specialists (GS-1084) and writers and editors (GS-1082).

GS-1100 BUSINESS AND INDUSTRY: Our government and the business world with which most of you are familiar have much in common. Both of these entities deal with contracts, property, purchasing, production and finances. Industrial production methods and processes, industrial and commercial contracts, and the examination and appraisal of merchandise or property are some of the business and trade activities of the government. Individuals with a working knowledge of advising, administering, supervising or performing this type of endeavor are needed. The occupations you'll find in this group include: agricultural marketing specialists (GS-1146), agricultural market reporters (GS-1147), agricultural program specialists (GS-1145), appraisers and assessors (GS-1171), business and industry specialists (GS-1101), commissary store managers (GS-1144), contract specialists (GS-1102), crop insurance administrators (GS-1161), financial analysts (GS-1160), housing managers (GS-1173), industrial property managers (GS-1103), industrial specialists (GS-1150), internal revenue officers (GS-1169), loan specialists (GS-1165), procurement clerks and assistants (GS-1106), production controllers (GS-1152), property disposal clerks and techs (GS-1107), property disposal specialists (GS-1104), public utilities specialists (GS-1l30), purchasing specialists (GS-1105), realtors (GS-1170) and trade specialists (GS-1140).

GS-1200 COPYRIGHT, PATENT AND TRADEMARK: At what point is an invention and invention? Who keeps track of all the designs, applications and details for copyright and patent approvals? The U.S. Patent Office within the Department of Commerce handles inquiries applications and recordkeeping functions in this area. Positions in this group include having the responsibilities for advising, administering, supervising, or performing professional scientific, technical and legal work related to copyright cataloging and registration; patent classification and issuance; and trademark registration. The occupations in this category include: patent attorneys (GS-1222) and patent examiners (GS-1224).

GS-1300 PHYSICAL SCIENCES: The physical world can be divided into three sections for scientific study: earth, water and space. The people employed in this group administer, supervise, advise or perform research, professional and scientific work or subordinate technical work in any of the science fields concerned with matter, energy, physical space, time, nature of physical measurement and the physical environment, and the fundamental structural particles. Occupations in this group include: astronomers and space scientists (GS-1330), cartographers (GS-1370), cartographic technicians (GS-1371), chemists (GS-1320), food technologists (GS-1382), general physical scientists (GS-1301), geodesists (GS-1372), geologists (GS-1350), geophysicists (GS-1313), health physicists (GS-1306), hydrologic technicians (Gs-1316), hydrologists (GS-1315), land surveyors (GS-1373), metallurgists (GS-1321), meteorological technicians (GS-1341), meteorologists (GS-1340), navigational information specialists (GS-1361), oceanographers (GS-1360), physical science technicians (GS-1311) and physicists (GS-1310).

GS-1400 LIBRARY AND ARCHIVES: The staff at any federal library helps to maintain the government's records in an up-to-date manner. People employed in this group work in the various phases of library and archival science and have responsibilities to supervise, administer, advise and perform professional and scientific work or ancillary technical work. The occupations in this field include: archivists (GS-1420), archives technicians (GS-1421), librarians (GS-1410), library techs (GS-1411) and technical information services specialists (GS-1412).

GS-1500 MATHEMATICS AND STATISTICS: Mathematics, statistics and financial principles apply in every facet of both our daily and business lives. This group has the responsibility for advising, administering, supervising and performing research or other professional and scientific work or related clerical work using mathematical principles, methods, procedures or relationships. Work in this group includes: actuaries (GS-1510), computer science specialists (GS-1550), mathematical statisticians (GS-1529), mathematicians (GS-1520), operations research analysts (GS-1515) and statisticians (GS-1530).

GS-1600 EQUIPMENT, FACILITIES AND SERVICE: Federally owned property is located all over the U.S. and world. A property site may include facilities, services and many time, buildings to be managed. Jobs in this group require technical or managerial skills and abilities, plus a practical knowledge of trades, crafts or manual labor operations. The people employed in this group must be able to advise, manage or instruct and inform others in such functions. The following occupations are included: cemetery superintendents (GS-1630), equipment specialists (GS-1670), facility managers (GS-1640), general facilities and equipment specialists (GS-1601), laundry and dry cleaning plant managers (GS-1658), printing specialists (GS-1654) and stewards (GS-1667).

GS-1700 EDUCATION: The federal government constantly trains new employees and supervisors and provides continuing refresher and retraining courses to its employees. The diversity in this area is tremendous. Jobs included are: educational program specialists (GS-1720), education and training specialists (GS-1701), education and training technicians (GS-1702), education and vocational training specialists (GS-1710), public health educators (GS-1725), training instructors (GS-1712) and vocational rehabilitation specialists (GS-1715).

GS-1800 INVESTIGATION: Ferreting out criminals, following clues, gathering and presenting evidence, watching people and merchandise entering the U.S., investigating prospective federal employees and working under cover are all duties within the investigation group. The federal government hires people for investigation, inspection and enforcement work to uphold and safeguard the laws, the people and the property of the U.S. Occupations in this group include: agricultural commodity warehouse examiners (GS-1850), air safety investigators (GS-1815), alcohol, tobacco, and firearms inspectors (GS-1854), aviation safety inspectors (GS-1825), border patrol agents (GS-1896), compliance inspection and support specialists (GS-1802), consumer safety inspectors (GS-1862), criminal investigators (GS-1811), customs aides (GS-1897), customs entry and liquidation specialists (GS-1894), customs inspectors (GS-1890), customs patrol officers (GS-1884), food inspectors (GS-1863), game law enforcement agents (GS-1812), general inspection, investigation and compliance specialists (GS-1801), general investigators (GS-1810), immigration inspectors (GS-1816), import specialists (GS-1889), mine safety and health inspectors (GS-1822) and securities compliance examiners (GS-1831).

GS-1900   QUALITY ASSURANCE, INSPECTION AND GRADING: Government operations demand quality products. Quality products depend on quality materials, facilities and processes. The federal government performs inspections and commodities grading to bring products up to standard levels. People working in this area must be well versed in quality assurance, inspection or commodities grading. The occupations included are: agricultural commodity aides (GS-1981), agricultural commodity graders (GS-1980)
and quality assurance specialists (GS-1910).

GS-2000 SUPPLY: It takes a myriad of goods and services to run the federal government. Every item is identified, selected and acquired, then it is counted, catalogued and distributed prior to being stored, inventoried or used. The jobs in this group require knowledge of one or more elements of supply systems, and /or supply methods, policies or procedures. Work performed within this group concerns the provision and control of supplies, equipment, material, property (excluding real estate) and other services to components of the federal government (or industrial or other concerns under contract to the government or receiving supplies from the government). The occupations in this group consist of: distribution facility and storage management specialists (GS-2030), inventory management specialists (GS-2010), packaging specialists (GS-2032), sales stores clerks (GS-2091), supply catalogers (GS-2050), supply clerks and technicians (GS-2005), supply program managers (GS-2003) and supply specialists (GS-2001).

GS-2100 TRANSPORTATION: The federal government requires many transportation services and regulates a variety of transportation activities. This group includes positions having responsibilities for advising, administering, supervising or performing clerical, administrative or technical work involved in providing transportation service to the government, regulating government transportation activities, or managing government funded transportation programs including research and development projects. The occupations in this group include: aircraft operators (GS-2181), air traffic assistants (GS-2154), air traffic controllers (GS-2152), cargo schedulers (GS-2144), dispatchers (GS-2151), freight rate specialists (GS-2131), highway safety specialists (GS-2125), marine cargo specialists (GS-2161), motor carrier safety specialists (GS-2123), railroad safety inspectors and specialists (GS-2121), shipment clerks and assistants (GS-2134), traffic management specialists (GS-2130), transportation clerks and assistants (GS-2102), transportation industry analysts (GS-2110), transportation loss damage claims examiners (GS-2135), transportation operators (GS-2150), transportation specialists (GS-2101) and travel assistants (GS-2132). **There are many employment opportunities available for air traffic controllers and assistants throughout the U.S.**

Well, there you have it. Amazed at the diversity of jobs available? Just about anyone reading these listings should see several jobs for which they are either qualified or of interest to them. We will talk at greater length later in this text about the specifics of each of the jobs mentioned, but for the time being this should give you an idea of just how extensive the government's needs are -- and where you may be able to fit in.

4.0 WHO TO CONTACT -- HOW TO GET HIRED

When applying for a federal job you will want to determine whether to file your application with an Office of Personnel Management (OPM) or directly to the agency doing the hiring. For jobs where one agency is the main employer, such as that of an Internal Revenue Agent working for the Treasury Department, the agency handles the hiring process on its own and will accept applications directly from applicants. Additionally, for occupations where there is a severe shortage of qualified workers, such as engineering, health and clerical jobs and transportation, individual agencies often conduct their own hiring and accept applications directly.

Likewise, for jobs that are common to many agencies, like accounting, computer specialists, etc, the OPM accepts applications, evaluates the candidates and then places the names of qualified individuals on a list for referral to agencies.

4.1 THE WRITTEN EXAM

Some government jobs require a written test. If a test is required for the kind of work you want, you will receive a notice telling you when and where to take the test. It is not necessary to prepare for the test by taking a "civil service" course. No school can guarantee that you will be found qualified or that you will be offered a job. If taking one of these courses, or reading texts that give sample exams puts your mind at ease with regard to actually taking the test -- then go for it! The idea is to get the job and whatever it takes for you to accomplish this goal will be worth the effort. You will, however, want to make sure you are not being taken advantage of financially.

Administrative Careers with America is the federal government's recruitment and examination program for its entry level administrative positions. Most of these positions require a written test. This program offers you the chance to compete and to be hired for one of the hundreds of challenging, entry-level administration positions that exist in federal offices across the U.S. and in some foreign countries. Approximately 100 different jobs are filled through this examination program. These positions start at the GS 5 and 7 grade levels. These are the typical grade levels at which baccalaureate graduates may enter the federal service. Under this program you can apply for federal service by taking one or more written exams or you can apply on the basis of your grade point average (GPA). **You do not need to be a college graduate to take the tests. You can use a combination of skills learned on the job and grades to meet entry level requirements.**

The governments entry-level administrative positions are divided into six broad occupational groups. Each occupational group has its own specific written exam. You can apply to take one or more exams based upon your education and work experience. The following is a list of the six groups:

Group 1: Health, Safety and Environmental Occupations.
Group 2: Writing and Public Information Occupations.
Group 3: Business, Finance and Management Occupations.
Group 4: Personnel, Administration and Computer Occupations.
Group 5: Benefits, Review, Tax and Legal Occupations.
Group 6: Law Enforcement and Investigation Occupations.

The second way to get an entry-level administrative position is based upon your grade point average. If you qualify on the basis of you GPA, you can bypass the written exams. If you are applying on the basis of your GPA, you must be a college graduate and have a GPA of 3.5 or higher, based on a 4.0 scale for all completed undergraduate course work, or have graduated in the upper ten percent of your class. You may apply for employment for an entry-level position under the Administrative Careers with America program when you are within nine months of graduation or completion of those academic courses qualifying you for the positions for which you wish to apply.

4.2 TELEPHONE HOTLINES

Many federal agencies have job information telephone hotlines and toll-free numbers that operate around the clock to provide employment information. When you are contacting an agency by phone, you should have a fairly good idea of the kind of job you are looking for. The federal government's central college hotline assists college students and graduates with employment, career and application information. **The hotline number is: (900) 990-9200.** You can call this number 24 hours a day, seven days a week. There is a charge of 40 cents a minute for each hotline call. Callers can leave voice-mail messages with their name, address and phone number. This information is processed daily and application packages are sent out within one day of OPM's staffing service center in Macon, Georgia.

Unlike many of the other government phone numbers, this 900 number is generally not busy. Once you get on line you will be easily guided through a series of questions which will allow you to gain the information you need.

4.3 THE FUTURE IS NOW - PHONE MODEMS TO ACCESS JOB INFO

If you have a computer with a phone modem you may be able to obtain federal job listings from the government's bulletin boards. The lists provide information about the vacancy, job title, job series number, grade level, opening and closing period for receipt of applications, job location, and where to obtain the necessary forms. This is a relatively new format being used by the government and currently has the following numbers you may wish to call. Again, you must have a phone modem and computer to use this information.

Current bulletin boards include: OPM Express/Dallas, TX (214) 729-0565; OPM Federal Jobs/Newark, NJ (201) 645-3887; OPM Atlanta/Atlanta,GA (404) 880-2370; Census Bureau/Suitland, MD (301) 763-4576; and Library of Congress/Washington, DC (202) 707-9656.

To access these bulletin boards you may have to fill out some forms and answer a few questions about your intended use. Additionally, you will want to remember that while this is a quick way to find out about jobs, it is pretty expensive, and you can obtain the same information in other ways at less expense.

FEDERAL JOB OPPORTUNITY LISTINGS (FJOL'S) include information about region-wide or nationwide vacancies. The FJOL's are posted at all Federal Job Information Centers and State employment offices.

4.4 AGENCIES AND POSITIONS OUTSIDE THE COMPETITIVE SERVICE

Most federal civil service jobs are in the competitive service, which means that people applying for them must compete with other applicants under rules set forth by the U.S. Office of Personnel Management. Candidates are selected on the basis of their ability to do the job. This ability must be shown either through education, experience or a written examination. A few agencies fill jobs which are in the excepted service or are outside the competitive service. To fill their positions, these agencies establish their own criteria for evaluating applicants. If you are interested in working for one of these agencies you will need to apply directly. The following list will give you information on how to locate these agencies:

Agency for International Development (A.I.D.)
Washington, DC 20523
Board of Governors of the Federal Reserve System
20th Street and Constitution Ave., NW
Washington, DC 20551

Central Intelligence Agency
P.O. Box 1925
Washington, DC 20013

Defense Intelligence Agency
Civilian Staffing Operations Division (RHR-2)
Washington, DC 20340-3042

Federal Bureau of Investigation
10th Street and Pennsylvania Ave., NW
Washington, DC 20520

General Accounting Office
Office of Recruitment
Room 4043-OD 441 G Street, NW
Washington, DC 20548

National Security Agency
Fort Meade, MD 20775

Nuclear Regulatory Commission
Office of Personnel
Washington, DC 20555

Postal Rate Commission
Administrative Office, Suite 300
1333 H Street, NW
Washington,DC 20268

Tennessee Valley Authority
Employment Services, ET 5C 50P-K
400 West Summit Hill Drive
Knoxville, TN 37902

U.S. Department of State (Foreign Service Positions)
Recruitment Division
P.O. Box 9317 Rosslyn Station
Arlington, VA 22209

In addition to being available at the Department of State, excepted Foreign Service positions exist in a number of other departments, agencies and organizations. For information on these excepted opportunities, contact should be made directly with each individual organization. Here are some contacts you may wish to make:

Foreign Agricultural Service
Department of Agriculture FAS Personnel
South Building
Washington, DC 20250-1000

United States and Foreign Commercial Service
Office of Foreign Service Personnel
Room 3226 International Trade Administration

Department of Commerce
Washington, DC   20230

United States Information Agency (USIA)
Office of Personnel/Special Services Branch
301 4th Street, SW
Washington, DC   20547

United States Mission to the United Nations
Personnel Office
799 United Nations Plaza
New York, NY   10017

Other excepted positions occur within the Judicial Branch of our government. The Judicial Branch includes all legal entities except the Administrative Office of the U.S. Courts and the U.S. Claims Court. For inquiries contact:

United States Supreme Court building
1 First Street, NW
Washington, DC   20543
(202) 479-3000

If you are interested in a job at the Administrative Office of the U.S. Courts and the U.S. Claims Court contact:

Administrative Office of the U.S. Courts
Personnel Division
Room L701
Washington, DC 20544

United States Claims Court
717 Madison Place, NW
Washington, DC 20005

The Legislative Branch also offers positions which are excepted . This branch includes Senators' and Representatives' offices, the Library of Congress, and the Capitol. Your inquiry should be submitted to:

The Senate Placement Office
The Capitol
Washington, DC   20510
(202) 224-9167

The House of Representatives Placement Office
The Capitol
Washington, DC   20515
(202) 226-6731

The Library of Congress Employment Office
LM-107
James Madison Memorial Building
101 Independence Avenue, SE
Washington, DC   20540

Even in agencies where most jobs are part of the competitive civil service, some jobs are excepted by law from Civil Service examination requirements. Congress has ruled that it is impractical to examine for such positions as attorney and chaplain.   Policy making positions and those jobs which require a close and confidential working relationship with people in policy-making positions are also excepted.   An examination is not required for any excepted position.

4.5 EMPLOYMENT PROGRAMS FOR SPECIAL GROUPS

The government has many special employment programs for individuals with disabilities, minorities, women and veterans. One of the goals of our government is to have a work force which reflects the diversity of the nation. In order to help achieve this goal, each federal agency has developed special recruiting and training programs aimed at attracting qualified women, Hispanics, African-Americans, American Indians, Alaska natives, Asians and Pacific Islanders.   The following is a brief look at each of these programs:

Federal Women's Program: This program promotes the employment of women in the federal service.   The primary focus is to attract women into key positions, especially into non-traditional occupations, and to promote programs which advance women within the federal work force.

Hispanic Employment Program: This program was established to attract Hispanic applicants for federal employment. Most federal agencies have Hispanic Employment Program Managers who provide assistance to Hispanic applicants. The federal government recognizes bilingual ability and knowledge of the Hispanic culture in evaluating qualification for those positions where these skills will enhance job performance.

Disabled Veterans Affirmative Action Program: This program tries to promote the hiring and advancement of disabled veterans by assisting them to find government jobs. Special employment considerations are made for disabled vets who have service-connected disabilities of 30 percent or greater. Every federal agency has outreach and training programs to help the disabled vet in his or her job search. Special appointing authorities and benefits are available for disabled veterans.

Selective Placement Program for Persons with Disabilities: Our government offers a wide array of recruiting, placement and training assistance to qualified persons with disabilities. Our government is one of the forerunners when it comes to providing reasonable accommodations which enable employees with disabilities to perform their duties. Opportunities are readily available for individuals who wish to excel.

Veterans Readjustment Appointment (VRA) Hiring Program: If you are a Vietnam Era veteran you may qualify to participate in this program. As a VRA participant you can receive job related training, education or both while working in your federal job. You may be eligible to receive a regular Civil Service appointment after two years of successful work. (See details in Chapter 6).

The Presidential Management Intern Program: This program works as the recruiting arm of the government for its future managers. The PMI program provides a first step toward an exciting and challenging career with the federal service. This program which was established by an Executive Order in 1977, is designed to "attract into the Federal Service outstanding individuals who have an interest in, and commitment to, a public service career."

You are eligible for the PMI program if you:

1. Are a citizen of the U.S. or expect to become a citizen prior to appointment.
2. Are scheduled to receive a graduate degree.
3. Have demonstrated an exceptional ability and a personal interest in a career in the analysis and management of public policies and programs.

Qualifying graduate degrees include a variety of academic disciplines. Following is a partial listing of study areas which qualify: accounting, information systems management, business administration, criminal justice, political science, economics, public administration, finance, public policy analysis, health administration, social services administration, international relations and urban planning.

PMI allows individuals to gain more than a job. It further gives them an opportunity to put what they know to work for their country. Qualified candidates are given a wide range of on-the-job training situations, as well as rotational opportunities within their chosen field. Individuals in this program are able to take advantage of regularly scheduled seminars, conferences and workshops.

It is necessary to be nominated for the PMI by the dean, director or chairperson of your graduate academic program. A competitive nomination process is devised by each school so that selections can be based on abilities, knowledge and skills -- after fair and open competition. Graduate school nominations must be submitted by December 1 each year.

To be considered for nomination a student must demonstrate academic excellence, the capacity for leadership, a high potential for future professional growth, and a commitment to and clear understanding of what it means to have a public service career.

Indian preference applies to all positions within the Bureau of Indian Affairs (BIA) of the U.S. Department of the Interior and the Indian Health Service (IHS) of the U.S. Department of Health and Human Services.

Students who are members of a federally recognized tribe and who are interested in pursuing employment with BIA or IHS should submit a certificate of blood quantum from their home agency in addition to the other forms required by the PMI program.

Final nominee selections are based on the following criteria:

1. Review of applicants and recommendations
2. Results of rigorous individual and group interviews
3. Evaluation of writing samples.

If you are chosen, your appointment may begin immediately upon completion of your graduate degree program.

Each PMI recipient receives an initial 2 year appointment. During the 2 year time period you are eligible for promotion. Upon completing the initial 2 year appointment your position will be converted to a permanent government position. At that time, you are eligible for further promotion. You will also be entitled to all civil service benefits, which include health and life insurance, retirement and investment plans, annual and sick leave, and assistance for additional career development. Most PMI recipients start at Grade 9, Step 1 ($26,798).

To apply for this program you should contact the head of your graduate program or your college placement office. Announcements inviting nominations to the PMI Program are mailed every September to graduate schools nationwide. Information can also be obtained at your nearest Federal Job Information Center. As a service to our readers, we have included a sample copy of the Institutional Nomination Forms and Application in Appendix 2 (page 105) for your review.

Cooperative Education: This is a planned and progressive educational program offering opportunities from high school through post graduate study. It combines your academic studies with on-the-job training to help you get the experience you'll need to move closer to getting the job you want.

This program allows you to take what you've learned in school and apply it in your every day work. It provides a means by which what you've learned in your books can have more meaning because you can see these examples in the work place. further, cooperative education gives you a chance to explore career options before you actually have to make a real choice on your life's work.

These co-op programs are designed to work with your school schedule. Some may alternate full-time work with full-time study. Others may provide for part-time work. The agencies, schools and students design a schedule that works best for them.

The federal government is the largest employer of co-op students in the country. Thousands of students participate at all academic levels. This program provides high quality work assignments to hopefully produce the managers, professionals and civil service workers for our government's future. Co-op students work across the country in a variety of setting. You might work in a lab, national forest, park, office, hospital, shipyard, etc. -- there are over 200 occupations from which to choose.

Co-op students begin earning a salary on their fist day of work. The initial rate of pay depends upon education and work experience. As you advance in responsibility, your pay is adjusted to recognize your knowledge and talents. Pay for performance systems have been established to provide increases and awards for motivated co-op students.

The benefits for which co-op students qualify include:

> paid vacation days, holidays and sick leave;
> major medical, dental and life insurance; and
> retirement/investment plans.

Co-op students may also be eligible for additional benefits such as: training and tuition assistance, reimbursement for transportation between school and work, and membership in an employee credit union.

Eligibility requirements include: pursuit of a professional, graduate, baccalaureate or associate degree, enrollment in your school's cooperative education program, good academic records, a recommendation for a co-op assignment from your school, and U.S. citizenship or a permanent resident who will be a citizen by graduation.

If you are interested in pursuing this program simply contact your school's Cooperative Education Director or Coordinator.

The Federal Junior Fellowship Program: This program is designed to give selected high school seniors the chance to earn money for college while they learn about their career choices through related work experience. This program allows its participants to work part-time while attending college and full-time during school breaks.

Junior Fellows are employed in positions which allow them to apply their academic studies to actual work experiences, thereby gaining first-hand knowledge of the federal government as an employer.

Eligibility requirements are as follows: you must be a graduating high school senior with a satisfactory academic record, either planning to attend or having already been accepted by a college or university. If your family income indicates the need for financial assistance (and these day, whose doesn't?) and you are a U.S. citizen or a national at the time of appointment, you've met all of the necessary requirements.

Each year in the late spring, federal agencies contact high schools across the U.S. to find out if the schools have nominations for this program. The recommendations are made by high school coordinators or guidance counselors. If you have been nominated and your name has been referred to a federal agency, then you may be contacted for an interview. When making final selections the agencies consider a number of factors -- academic achievement, financial need, intended college major, career goals, extra-curricular activities and teacher recommendations.

Those selected for this program start work immediately after they graduate from high school. Federal Junior Fellows' rate of pay is based on their current education and work experience. As an individual advances in responsibility, their pay takes into account their contributions and talents. Junior Fellows are eligible for the following benefits: paid vacation days and holidays and sick leave; a choice of major medical, dental and life insurance; retirement/investment plans; and training and tuition assistance.

If you or a family member are interested in this program, you should talk to the guidance counselor at your high school about the application process.

The Stay In School Program: This program is designed to provide financially needy, or students with disabilities, employment opportunities in the federal government.

As a Stay In School participant you are allowed to work part time while school is in session and full-time during school breaks.

Intermittent schedules can also be arranged for people who are unable to work under a fixed part time schedule. An intermittent schedule is one where you work on an "as needed" basis.

The eligibility requirements for this program are as follows:

1. Enrollment as a full time student in an accredited high school, vocational school or baccalaureate program;
2. Working toward a degree, diploma or certificate;
3. Maintaining a satisfactory academic record;
4. At least 16 years of age at the time of appointment;
5. A U.S. citizen, or a national at the time of appointment;
6. In need of earnings (except those qualifying as disabled students) and qualified under the financial needs criteria based on family income.

As a Stay in Schooler, your rate of pay will depend on your current education and work experience. As you advance, you will be eligible for promotions, awards, and other pay increases. Additionally, you are entitled to other benefits including paid vacation days, holidays and sick leave.

Each year about 20,000 students participate in this program. Agencies recruit candidates directly from schools or through local state employment or job service offices. You can contact your school or the offices mentioned above for assistance in getting started.

The Summer Employment and Summer Aid Programs: The Summer Employment Program creates training and work opportunities for persons who can only work during the summer months. These positions begin in mid-May and usually end September 30th. The work ranges from office support and trades and labor occupations to positions in professional fields.

To be eligible you must be at least 16 years of age and qualify for the position based on experience and/or education.

The Summer Aid program is designed to provide summer jobs for economically disadvantaged or disabled youths. Youth's employed under this program have the opportunity to make use of the skills they already possess, and gain special training and on-the-job experience to enable them to gain new skills.

To qualify for positions under the Summer Aid program you must:

1. Be at least 16 years of age; and
2. Be in need of earnings (except those who qualify as a disabled student) and qualify under the financial needs criteria based upon family income.

Anyone interested in this program can get further information by registering with the State Employment or Job Service Office in their area. Information can also be obtained by getting a copy of the Government's Summer Jobs Announcement, No. 414. This announcement is available each December through the Federal Job Information Centers throughout the U.S. Deadlines for applying for these summer jobs are set by the individual agencies participating in the program.

The Student Volunteer Program: The Student Volunteer Program is an unpaid work opportunity which provides students with a chance to explore various occupations. Student volunteers are exposed to the federal work environment to see if they develop interests in new or emerging occupations and professions. If you, or someone you know, are enrolled in an accredited high school or trade school (even if it's only part time); junior college; technical or vocational school; or four year college or university you qualify.

You, your school, and the federal agency for which you volunteer determine the work schedule best suited to meet your needs. Some schools even award academic credit for the volunteer work you perform. Additionally, your volunteer service may be considered as related work experience when you later apply for permanent employment with the federal government. If you are interested in this program, talk to your counselor at school, or get in touch with the federal agency you wish to volunteer.

5.0 EVERYTHING YOU NEED TO KNOW ABOUT THE SF-171

If you want to work for the federal government, you're going to have to become familiar with the SF-171 form. The SF-171 is the standard application form used by the federal government. You can obtain one from any Federal Job Information Center, federal agency personnel office, state employment services or college placement office. We have included a sample form in this book so that you can familiarize yourself with the form and the information it requires you to complete. It is important that you fill out this application accurately and completely because the information you provide will be used to evaluate you for most federal employment. If at all possible, type the form or have someone type it for you, making sure there are no mistakes or typographical errors. Remember, this is the first impression you will be making -- so you want it to be good!

In most instances you will want to fill your application out with a specific occupation or position in mind. Therefore, you should analyze your work experience and qualifications and decide how they match the requirements of a position. There may be situations where you will want to complete the SF-171 without a specific position in mind, but you will always want to have at least a general idea of the kind of work you are seeking.

Prior to filling out the application form you should gather and/or study these items:

1. The vacancy announcement (when you are applying for a specific vacancy);
2. The X-118 Handbook which lists the qualification standards for a particular job (this handbook is usually available in your public library);
3. A supply of SF-171 forms plus any other supplementary forms that may be required
4. A list of the selective and/or desirable elements for the job so that you can directly relate your experience to these factors;
5. Any records of your achievements, awards, training, hobbies, etc.;
6. Explanations of all your work related experiences -- even volunteer work.

Your SF-171 should be concise and well organized. You don't want to include information that is unrelated to your qualifications for a vacancy. Make sure you list all items in some logical manner so that the information flows in an orderly manner. Clearly describe your background, making sure to eliminate unnecessary data. You want to pay close attention to completely describing your abilities and accomplishments. It should take you a couple of hours to thoroughly complete your SF-171 form. It is acceptable for you to cut and paste your form to tailor it so that the blocks for information are large enough for you to include all of the necessary information. If you do cut and paste, make sure it is done neatly and in the same sequence as the original form.

5.1 AN ITEM BY ITEM OVERVIEW OF THE SF-171

Item 1: Leave this blank on the original. Complete this block when you are applying for a specific position or a specific announcement.

Items 1-9: These are pretty much self-explanatory. If any of your experience or education is under another name, make sure you give this information in Item 7 and at the appropriate place by putting the previous name in parentheses at the end of each work or education description to which it applies.

Item 10: If you mark yes, write the highest grade you have ever held, along with the series, job title, and the dates you were in that grade.

Items 11: Leave blank on your original. Fill in the month and year that you will be available on the copy to be submitted. Don't use ASAP. Indicate that you are willing to give at least two weeks notice!

Item 12: Leave blank on your original. When applying for a specific job, fill in the grade level(s) shown on the announcement. If applying to U.S. OPM, put in the entire range of grades for the register you are applying. Each category of register is maintained separately at the U.S. OPM. You must submit a separate SF-171 for each register. You will not be considered for levels lower than you indicate, but you will be considered for higher.

Items 13-16: Accepting a temporary position will not exclude you from being considered for permanent positions. Make sure you don't forget to check your availability for overnight travel. If the position you are applying for requires travel and you indicate you are not available for travel, even overnight occasionally, you will not be considered. If you are willing to accept a temporary assignment (especially if you are currently unemployed) it can be a good way of getting your foot in the door for a permanent job. Temporary jobs give you an opportunity to prove your abilities -- and to show that you are willing to do whatever it takes to get work.

Items 17-22: If you are a veteran, enter factual information about your status. Read the instructions carefully to determine whether or not you qualify for preference under the rules for vets.

Item 23: Check "yes" only if you are willing to have your present employer contacted regarding your character, qualifications, and work record.

Item 24: **THIS IS THE MOST IMPORTANT PART OF YOUR SF-171!** If you neglect to provide all of the information requested in this section it could cause you to be disqualified for the position. Make sure you are thorough and concise. Don't substitute copes of your position description. Duties are what you do for your employer. Responsibilities involve some independence and judgment on your part. Accomplishments are what you have done that is above and beyond the normal parameters of the job. Make sure you go over your draft description keeping the above guidelines in mind. Make your duties sound interesting and challenging. Using action verbs will help you to convey a bit more excitement.

Each item of your work experience should be ranked according to its importance. Once you have accomplished this task review your list to see which ones pertain to the job you are seeking. If they enhance your qualifications and your competitiveness for the job include them, otherwise don't. After you take a look at your list, only your important duties, responsibilities and accomplishments should remain. Be honest, don't make statements you can't back up. Dishonesty will destroy your chances of getting work.

Once you've organized your experience and defined your duties, responsibilities, and accomplishments, emphasize and highlight the portions of your descriptions which enhance evidence that you have progressed in each job and from one job to the next. Make sure you outline how you have assumed more responsibilities or more demanding tasks with each job.

If you have ever done volunteer work be sure to include this information. Write each description as though you were talking about experience in a paying job. Make your descriptions specific. Emphasize relevant skills. Enter this information in separate blocks.

Explain your experiences in reverse chronological order, beginning in Block A with your present job. Describe in Block B the position you held before that, and continue to work backwards. Identify each experience block, using separate blocks for each employer, promotion, substantial salary change, job reassignment, or detail. If it is not pertinent to your current career, summarize experience gained more than 15 years ago into one experience block.

If you currently supervise or have supervised other employees, make sure you include the number and grades of the employees you have supervised, giving details on your duties as a supervisor.

The length of the description depends on the information which is pertinent to the type of job you are seeking. Your goal should be to have as complete, relevant and readable a statement of your experience as possible.

If you are currently in school and unemployed, write "See block 25" for current school activity. If you are involved in an unpaid or volunteer activity, describe it fully. If you are a homemaker and not involved in any unpaid volunteer work or educational activity, write "homemaker", then go to Block B. As a homemaker, you have much valuable experience in the running of one our most important businesses -- the family. You have learned to budget in ways that allow for your family to survive economically, allowing for daily needs and major purchases. Believe it or not, when you are applying for work this experience can be translated into work experience. It is important that you not hesitate to include a brief description of the experiences you have gained over the years you've cared for your family and managed a household.

Items 25-31: Be sure to provide all of the information requested. Any degrees you expect to receive within nine months of the date of your application can also be included. Life experiences may also provide you with the necessary growth and development needed to enhance your skill levels and abilities -- these may be credited to you even if you don't have a college background. For those of you with little work experience, you can substitute education for experience. So you see, there is something for everyone.

On item 31 you'll want to provide all of the following:

1. School name and location (city, state and zip code).
2. Month and year training was completed, including number of classroom hours.
3. Subjects studied.
4. Whether training was completed.

Make certain you list the courses in reverse chronological order, starting with the most current one first. Include correspondence courses, if pertinent, stating whether the course is accredited. Don't forget to include training courses you may have taken, regardless of their length. The fact you've participated in these types of courses shows a willingness on your part to enhance your skills.

Items 32-35: Your response to these questions could be the deciding factors on whether a prospective employer hires you or another applicant who may be equally qualified. It is important that you indicate any special qualification, skills and accomplishments, i.e. writing experience, publications, public speaking ability, hobbies which specifically relate to the position you are seeking, memberships and professional affiliations, etc. Don't be modest. Make sure you blow your own horn on this occasion! If you've been nominated for offices, given commendations, awards or certificates -- let them know.

Confused about what to include? Here are some guidelines to help:

MEMBERSHIPS AND PROFESSIONAL AFFILIATIONS: List any relevant professional, civic and scholarly organizations, past and present. Give exact dates where applicable. Professionals are often expected to belong to professional organizations. If you are not a member -- join now. If your involvement in these organizations is extensive, make sure this is duly noted. If you hold an office, that's important information to include.

WRITING: Writing samples need not be copyrighted publications. Make a complete list of any titles, including reports, guides, handbooks, instructions, pamphlets and other material which you have authored, including the date and any other important information. If you are applying for a job as a Writer/Editor, you'll want to list only your primary publications.

PUBLIC SPEAKING: If you've ever presented a report to a club, taught a Sunday school class or delivered a speech, but sure to include this information. You don't have to be a polished speaker. If you are a member of a toastmasters group, put this down. List any experience where you've had to persuade, teach, or brief an audience. Keep your list brief and to the point. If public speaking is part of your career, make sure you present only the key points, i.e. 10 presentations of "New Technology in the Work Place" as guest lecturer at city colleges and high schools.

HOBBIES: As mentioned above, list only those hobbies which directly relate to the job for which you are applying. If you're an amateur photographer applying for a job requiring a background in photography, this is worth mentioning! If you make quilts in your spare time and you're applying for a job as a photographer, it's not going to change any minds when the hiring decision is made.

TYPING SKILLS: These skills are highly important if you are seeking a position as a secretary/clerk or a writer/editor, researcher, or other position where typing is an asset. Word processing and microcomputer skills are an asset for many professional and administrative jobs and should definitely be mentioned in Item 32 under the heading "Skills with machines."

Item 35: If the position you desire requires a proficiency in a foreign language you will most likely be required to take an examination. If your language skills are limited to what you remember from your sophomore year of high school, you'd be better off not listing any language for most jobs.

Item 36: Provide the names of three (3) people who are not related to you, who are not named as supervisors in your experience blocks, and who know of your qualifications and fitness for the job. These can be former or current co-workers -- as long as they are willing to be contacted. Always check with your references prior to using them to get their approval. This is also a good way to make sure the addresses and numbers you have for them are current. You'll want to provide both their home and work numbers so they can be easily contacted.

Items 37 - 44: While these questions are highly personal, it's important you answer them truthfully, as a dishonest answer can be grounds for dismissal at some future date.

Item 45: Be concise, simply state information which will clarify your answer to one of the questions in Items 37-44.

Items 46 - 47: Self-explanatory. Answer as completely as possible.

Item 48: **Once you've completed your SF-171 save the original. Do not sign the original, but make clear, legible copies.** As you apply for jobs, fill in items 1 and 2 appropriately. SIGN AND DATE EACH COPY AS YOU USE IT. This is very important because an agency will no accept a 171 with a photocopied signature or one which is dated in advance of the job announcement. When you submit your SF-171 put it in a full sized envelope for mailing. NEVER USE A GOVERNMENT PREPAID PENALTY ENVELOPE. Not only is it illegal, but some agencies will throw away applications received in government envelopes.

If you need more space for any of the items we've mentioned, use full sheets of paper the same size as the SF-171. Write on the top of each sheet your name and social security number, as well as the examination or position title and the announcement number.

Don't forget -- the SF-171 provides a history of you. As you change jobs, receive more training, or assume new responsibilities, include this data on your SF-171. Additionally, if the requirements vary for the different positions for which you apply, make sure to revise your SF-171 to suit each job.

Application for Federal Employment—SF 171

Read the instructions before you complete this application. *Type or print clearly in dark ink.*

Form Approved
OMB No 3206-0012

GENERAL INFORMATION

1 What kind of job are you applying for? *Give title and announcement no. (if any)*

2 Social Security Number

3 Sex
- [ ] Male
- [ ] Female

4 Birth date *(Month, Day, Year)*

5 Birthplace *(City and State or Country)*

6 Name *(Last, First, Middle)*

Mailing address *(include apartment number, if any)*

City   State   ZIP Code

7 Other names ever used *(e.g., maiden name, nickname, etc.)*

8 Home Phone
Area Code | Number

9 Work Phone
Area Code | Number | Extension

10 Were you ever employed as a civilian by the Federal Government? If "NO", go to Item 11. If "YES", mark each type of job you held with an "X".
- [ ] Temporary
- [ ] Career-Conditional
- [ ] Career
- [ ] Excepted

What is your **highest** grade, classification series and job title?

Dates at highest grade: FROM _____ TO _____

FOR USE OF EXAMINING OFFICE ONLY

Date entered register | Form reviewed:
Form approved:

Option	Grade	Earned Rating	Veteran Preference	Augmented Rating
			[ ] No Preference Claimed	
			[ ] 5 Points (Tentative)	
			[ ] 10 Pts (30% Or More Comp Dis)	
			[ ] 10 Pts (Less Than 30% Comp Dis)	
			[ ] Other 10 Points	

Initials and Date

[ ] Disallowed   [ ] Being Investigated

FOR USE OF APPOINTING OFFICE ONLY

Preference has been verified through proof that the separation was under honorable conditions, and other proof as required.

- [ ] 5-Point
- [ ] 10-Point—30% or More Compensable Disability
- [ ] 10-Point—Less Than 30% Compensable Disability
- [ ] 10-Point—Other

Signature and Title

Agency _____ Date _____

AVAILABILITY

11 When can you start work? *(Month and Year)*

12 What is the **lowest** pay you will accept? *(You will not be considered for jobs which pay less than you indicate.)*

Pay $ _____ per _____ OR Grade _____

13 In what geographic area(s) are you willing to work?

14 Are you willing to work:

	YES	NO
A. 40 hours per week *(full-time)*?		
B. 25-32 hours per week *(part-time)*?		
C. 17-24 hours per week *(part-time)*?		
D. 16 or fewer hours per week *(part-time)*?		
E. An intermittent job *(on-call/seasonal)*?		
F. Weekends, shifts, or rotating shifts?		

15 Are you willing to take a temporary job lasting:

A. 5 to 12 months *(sometimes longer)*?		
B. 1 to 4 months?		
C. Less than 1 month?		

16 Are you willing to travel away from home for:

A. 1 to 5 nights each month?		
B. 6 to 10 nights each month?		
C. 11 or more nights each month?		

MILITARY SERVICE AND VETERAN PREFERENCE

17 Have you served in the United States Military Service? *If your only active duty was training in the Reserves or National Guard, answer "NO". If "NO", go to item 22.*   YES | NO

18 Did you or will you retire at or above the rank of major or lieutenant commander?   YES | NO

MILITARY SERVICE AND VETERAN PREFERENCE (Cont.)

19 Were you discharged from the military service under honorable conditions? *(If your discharge was changed to "honorable" or "general" by a Discharge Review Board, answer "YES". If you received a clemency discharge, answer "NO".)* If "NO", provide below the date and type of discharge you received.   YES | NO

Discharge Date *(Month, Day, Year)*	Type of Discharge

20 List the dates *(Month, Day, Year)*, and branch for all **active duty** military service.

From	To	Branch of Service

21 If all your active military duty was after October 14, 1976, list the full names and dates of all campaign badges or expeditionary medals you received or were entitled to receive.

22 Read the instructions that came with this form before completing this item. When you have determined your eligibility for veteran preference from the instructions, place an "X" in the box next to your veteran preference claim.

- [ ] NO PREFERENCE
- [ ] 5-POINT PREFERENCE -- You must show proof when you are hired.

10-POINT PREFERENCE -- If you claim 10-point preference, place an "X" in the box below next to the basis for your claim. **To receive 10-point preference you must also complete a Standard Form 15, Application for 10-Point Veteran Preference, which is available from any Federal Job Information Center. ATTACH THE COMPLETED SF 15 AND REQUESTED PROOF TO THIS APPLICATION.**

- [ ] Non-compensably disabled or Purple Heart recipient.
- [ ] Compensably disabled, less than 30 percent.
- [ ] Spouse, widow(er), or mother of a deceased or disabled veteran.
- [ ] Compensably disabled, 30 percent or more.

PREVIOUS EDITION USABLE UNTIL 12-31-90

NSN 7540-00-935-7150   171-109

Standard Form 171 (Rev. 6-88)
U.S. Office of Personnel Management
FPM Chapter 295

Page 1

23 May we ask your present employer about your character, qualifications, and work record? A "NO" will not affect our review of your qualifications. If you answer "NO" and we need to contact your present employer before we can offer you a job, we will contact you first. ....

YES NO

24 READ **WORK EXPERIENCE** IN THE INSTRUCTIONS BEFORE YOU BEGIN

- Describe your current or most recent job in Block A and work backwards, describing each job you held **during the past 10 years.** If you were **unemployed** for longer than **3 months** within the past 10 years, list the dates and your address(es) in an experience block.

- You may sum up in one block work that you did **more than 10 years ago.** But if that work **is related** to the type of job you are applying for, describe each related job in a separate block.

- INCLUDE VOLUNTEER WORK *(non-paid work)*--If the work *(or a part of the work)* **is like the job you are applying for,** complete all parts of the experience block just as you would for a paying job. You may receive credit for work experience with religious, community, welfare, service, and other organizations.

- INCLUDE MILITARY SERVICE--You should complete **all** parts of the experience block just as you would for a non-military job, including all supervisory experience. Describe each major change of duties or responsibilities in a separate experience block

- IF YOU NEED MORE SPACE TO DESCRIBE A JOB--Use sheets of paper the same size as this page (be sure to include all information we ask for in **A** and **B** below). On **each** sheet show your name, Social Security Number, and the announcement number or job title.

- IF YOU NEED MORE EXPERIENCE BLOCKS, use the SF 171-A or a sheet of paper

- IF YOU NEED TO UPDATE (ADD MORE RECENT JOBS), use the SF 172 or a sheet of paper as described above

A | Name and address of employer's organization *(include ZIP Code, if known)* | Dates employed *(give month, day and year)* | Average number if hours per week | Number of employees you supervise

From: To:

Salary or earnings | Your reason for wanting to leave

Starting $ per

Ending $ per

Your immediate supervisor | Exact title of your job | If Federal employment *(civilian or military)* list series, grade or rank, and, if promoted in this job, the date of your last promotion

Name | Area Code | Telephone No

Description of work: Describe your specific duties, responsibilities and accomplishments in this job, including the job title(s) of any employees you supervise. *If you describe more than one type of work (for example, carpentry and painting, or personnel and budget), write the approximate percentage of time you spent doing each*

For Agency Use (skill codes, etc.)

B | Name and address of employer's organization *(include ZIP Code, if known)* | Dates employed *(give month, day and year)* | Average number of hours per week | Number of employees you supervised

From: To:

Salary or earnings | Your reason for leaving

Starting $ per

Ending $ per

Your immediate supervisor | Exact title of your job | If Federal employment *(civilian or military)* list series, grade or rank, and, if promoted in this job, the date of your last promotion

Name | Area Code | Telephone No

Description of work: Describe your specific duties, responsibilities and accomplishments in this job, including the job title(s) of any employees you supervised. *If you describe more than one type of work (for example, carpentry and painting, or personnel and budget), write the approximate percentage of time you spent doing each*

For Agency Use (skill codes, etc.)

Page 2 IF YOU NEED MORE EXPERIENCE BLOCKS, USE SF 171-A *(SEE BACK OF INSTRUCTION PAGE).*

EDUCATION

25 Did you graduate from high school? *If you have a GED high school equivalency or will graduate within the next nine months, answer "YES".*

26 Write the name and location *(city and state)* of the last high school you attended or where you obtained your GED high school equivalency.

YES ▸ If "YES", give month and year graduated
NO ▸ or received GED equivalency: .... _____
If "NO", give the highest grade you completed: _____

27 Have you ever attended college or graduate school?
YES ▸ If "YES", continue with 28.
NO ▸ If "NO", go to 31.

28 NAME AND LOCATION *(city, state and ZIP Code)* OF COLLEGE OR UNIVERSITY. *If you expect to graduate within nine months, give the month and year you expect to receive your degree:*

Name	City	State	ZIP Code	MONTH AND YEAR ATTENDED From	To	NUMBER OF CREDIT HOURS COMPLETED Semester	Quarter	TYPE OF DEGREE *(e.g. B.A., M.A.)*	MONTH AND YEAR OF DEGREE
1)									
2)									
3)									

29

CHIEF UNDERGRADUATE SUBJECTS *Show major on the first line*	NUMBER OF CREDIT HOURS COMPLETED Semester	Quarter
1)		
2)		
3)		

30

CHIEF GRADUATE SUBJECTS *Show major on the first line*	NUMBER OF CREDIT HOURS COMPLETED Semester	Quarter
1)		
2)		
3)		

31 If you have completed any **other courses or training related to the kind of jobs you are applying for** *(trade, vocational, Armed Forces, business)* give information below.

NAME AND LOCATION *(city, state and ZIP Code)* OF SCHOOL	MONTH AND YEAR ATTENDED From	To	CLASS-ROOM HOURS	SUBJECT(S)	TRAINING COMPLETED YES	NO
School Name 1)						
City State ZIP Code						
School Name 2)						
City State ZIP Code						

SPECIAL SKILLS, ACCOMPLISHMENTS AND AWARDS

32 Give the title and year of any honors, awards or fellowships you have received. List your special qualifications, skills or accomplishments that may help you get a job. *Some examples are: skills with computers or other machines; most important publications (do not submit copies); public speaking and writing experience; membership in professional or scientific societies; patents or inventions; etc.*

33 How many words per minute can you:
TYPE? TAKE DICTATION?

Agencies may test your skills before hiring you.

34 List **job-related** licenses or certificates that you have, such as: *registered nurse; lawyer; radio operator; driver's; pilot's; etc.*

LICENSE OR CERTIFICATE	DATE OF LATEST LICENSE OR CERTIFICATE	STATE OR OTHER LICENSING AGENCY
1)		
2)		

35 Do you speak or read a language other than English *(include sign language)?* *Applicants for jobs that require a language other than English may be given an interview conducted solely in that language.*
YES ▸ If "YES", list each language and place an "X" in each column that applies to you.
NO ▸ If "NO", go to 36.

LANGUAGE(S)	CAN PREPARE AND GIVE LECTURES Fluently	With Difficulty	CAN SPEAK AND UNDERSTAND Fluently	Passably	CAN TRANSLATE ARTICLES Into English	From English	CAN READ ARTICLES FOR OWN USE Easily	With Difficulty
1)								
2)								

REFERENCES

36 List three people who are not related to you and are not supervisors you listed under **24** who know your qualifications and fitness for the kind of job for which you are applying. At least **one** should know you well on a personal basis.

FULL NAME OF REFERENCE	TELEPHONE NUMBER(S) *(Include Area Code)*	PRESENT BUSINESS OR HOME ADDRESS *(Number, street and city)*	STATE	ZIP CODE
1)				
2)				
3)				

Page 3

37 Are you a citizen of the United States? *(In most cases you must be a U.S. citizen to be hired. You will be required to submit proof of* | YES | NO
identity and citizenship at the time you are hired.)* If **"NO"**, give the country or countries you are a citizen of: _____

> **NOTE: It is important that you give complete and truthful answers to questions 38 through 44.** If you answer **"YES"** to any of them, provide your explanation(s) in **Item 45. Include** convictions resulting from a plea of nolo contendere *(no contest)*. **Omit:** 1) traffic fines of $100.00 or less; 2) any violation of law committed before your 16th birthday; 3) any violation of law committed before your 18th birthday, if finally decided in juvenile court or under a Youth Offender law; 4) any conviction set aside under the Federal Youth Corrections Act or similar State law; 5) any conviction whose record was expunged under Federal or State law. We will consider the date, facts, and circumstances of each event you list. In most cases you can still be considered for Federal jobs. However, **if you fail to tell the truth or fail to list all relevant** events or circumstances, this may be grounds for not hiring you, for firing you after you begin work, or for criminal prosecution (18 USC 1001).

		YES	NO
38	During the last **10 years**, were you **fired from any job** for any reason, did you **quit after being told that you would be fired**, or did you leave by mutual agreement because of specific problems?.		
39	Have you **ever** been convicted of, or forfeited collateral for **any felony violation?** *(Generally, a felony is defined as any violation of law punishable by imprisonment of longer than one year, except for violations called misdemeanors under State law which are punishable by imprisonment of two years or less.)*		
40	Have you **ever** been convicted of, or forfeited collateral for **any firearms or explosives violation?**		
41	Are you **now** under charges for **any** violation of law?		
42	During the **last 10 years** have you forfeited collateral, been convicted, been imprisoned, been on probation, or been on parole? Do **not** include violations reported in 39, 40, or 41, above.		
43	Have you **ever** been convicted by a military **court-martial?** If no military service, answer **"NO"**.		
44	Are you **delinquent** on any Federal debt? *(Include delinquencies arising from Federal taxes, loans, overpayment of benefits, and other debts to the U.S. Government **plus** defaults on Federally guaranteed or insured loans such as student and home mortgage loans.)*		

45 If **"YES"** in: **38** - Explain for each job the problem(s) and your reason(s) for leaving. Give the employer's name and address.

39 through 43 - Explain each violation. Give place of occurrence and name/address of police or court involved.

44 - Explain the type, length and amount of the delinquency or default, and steps you are taking to correct errors or repay the debt. Give any identification number associated with the debt and the address of the Federal agency involved.

NOTE: If you need more space, use a sheet of paper, and include the item number.

Item No.	Date (Mo./Yr.)	Explanation	Mailing Address
			Name of Employer, Police, Court, or Federal Agency
			City State ZIP Code
			Name of Employer, Police, Court, or Federal Agency
			City State ZIP Code

		YES	NO
46	Do you receive, or have you ever applied for retirement pay, pension, or other pay based on military, Federal civilian, or District of Columbia Government service?		
47	Do any of your relatives work for the United States Government or the United States Armed Forces? Include: *father; mother; husband; wife; son; daughter; brother; sister; uncle; aunt; first cousin; nephew; niece; father-in-law; mother-in-law; son-in-law; daughter-in-law; brother-in-law; sister-in-law; stepfather; stepmother; stepson; stepdaughter; stepbrother; stepsister; half brother; and half sister.*		

If **"YES"**, provide details below. If you need more space, use a sheet of paper.

Name	Relationship	Department, Agency or Branch of Armed Forces

SIGNATURE, CERTIFICATION, AND RELEASE OF INFORMATION

YOU MUST SIGN THIS APPLICATION.   Read the following carefully before you sign.

- A false statement on any part of your application may be grounds for not hiring you, or for firing you after you begin work. Also, you may be punished by fine or imprisonment (U.S. Code, title 18, section 1001).
- If you are a male born after December 31, 1959 you must be registered with the Selective Service System or have a valid exemption in order to be eligible for Federal employment. You will be required to certify as to your status at the time of appointment.
- I **understand** that any information I give may be investigated as allowed by law or Presidential order.
- I **consent** to the release of information about my ability and fitness for Federal employment by *employers, schools, law enforcement agencies and other individuals and organizations,* to *investigators, personnel staffing specialists, and other authorized employees of the Federal Government.*
- I **certify** that, to the best of my knowledge and belief, **all** of my statements are true, correct, complete, and made in good faith.

48 SIGNATURE *(Sign each application in dark ink)*	**49** DATE SIGNED *(Month, day, year)*

*U.S. Government Printing Office: 1988-241-175/80208

6.0 HOW TO INTERVIEW FOR A JOB

During your search for government employment you will likely have more than one interview. You may be called upon to interview in a government office, on a college campus, at a job fair -- or even over the telephone.

It is crucial that you be prepared for the interviews. Here are a few helpful tips which apply to any interview situation:

1. Know your career goals. If you are unsure of what you want to do, you are not likely to present yourself as professionally as you might otherwise.
2. Make sure you speak clearly.
3. Don't get so caught up in what you are saying that you forget to listen carefully to questions you are being asked.
4. You only get one first impression. Make sure you are neatly dressed and groomed.
5. Be on time.
6. Make sure you have some questions you want to ask during the interview. You don't want the interview to be one sided.
7. Be ready to answer questions about yourself. Make positive and accurate statements about your abilities. Don't dwell on weaknesses.
8. Don't interrupt the interviewer.
9. Never, repeat, never, criticize your present or former supervisors or employers. If you are/were dissatisfied with your job (or former job) you may have legitimate reasons for feeling the way you do -- you will, however, look less than professional and ethical if you choose to publicly display your dirty laundry.
10. Don't volunteer negative information about yourself. This doesn't mean you should lie about anything -- just don't volunteer information unless you are specifically asked to do so.
11. Regardless of how casual the interview may feel, remember that you must always present yourself in a professional manner.

6.1 THE TWO TYPES OF INTERVIEWS

There are two types of interviews you may be asked to attend. One is the information interview in which you obtain information about your potential job market and develop a network of contacts. In the job interview you provide information to an employer about yourself and obtain information about a specific opening and agency.

The Information Interview: The purpose of this type of an interview is for you to obtain information which will assist you in finding work. Usually, it will be up to you to initiate this type of interview with people who are knowledgeable about career opportunities in your field. Your information interviews will be most successful if you keep the following in mind:

1. Identify your career goals.
2. When calling to set up an interview make sure the person you will be talking to knows you don't expect them to be able to give you a job -- or even tell you about jobs that may be open.
3. Have a prepared list of questions about your field of interest.
4. Let the interviewer know why you are seeking his or her help.
5. Ask the interviewer to review your SF-171 so they can suggest ways in which you can improve it.
6. Ask for the names of government managers and other people you might be able to contact to gather more information about your field of interest.
7. Don't forget to send a thank you letter for their time and assistance.

The Job Interview: You will be well prepared for a job interview if you know yourself and what you want to do as thoroughly as possible. Before your interview try to find out as much as you can about the person who will be doing the interview and the agency. Listen actively. Show enthusiasm. If you don't understand something, don't be afraid to ask.

Here are some of the questions you may be asked during an interview. How would you answer them?

1. Tell me about your background?
2. Why do you want a job with this agency?
3. Why are you leaving (or did you leave) your present job?
4. How can you contribute to this agency?
5. What are your strengths and weaknesses?
6. Why do you want this job?
7. Where do you see yourself in five years?
8. What would you like to know about the job?
9. What questions do you have about this department or agency?
10. When will you be available for work?
11. What salary do you expect?
12. Why haven't you obtained a job yet?
13. Will you be willing to work overtime?
14. What do (did) you like best about your present job?
15. What do (did) you like least?

6.2 WHY PEOPLE DON'T GET JOBS

Here are some of the most frequent reasons why people are not hired for a job:

1.   Poor personal appearance and inappropriate mannerisms during the interview.

It is imperative that you dress neatly and professionally. You wouldn't believe how many people go on a job interview dressed in levis, shorts, halter tops, sandals, etc. While you may not always be required to wear suits or dressy clothes once you have a job -- it is very important that during your interview you show the respect necessary to be considered.

2.   Acting uncertain of how to answer a question. If you portray to your interviewer that you are either trying to hide something -- or simply don't know the correct way in which to answer a question, you will raise questions in their mind about your competence.

3.   Lack of enthusiasm or vitality. If you go on a job interview and act like you're being put out, the interviewer is not going to be left with a favorable impression. Who would you rather hire, someone who is vibrant and thoughtful, or someone who slouches down in their chair and mumbles his or her answers?

4.   Lack of preparation or planning. A great example of this is going to an interview and when asked for someone's phone number having to ask the interviewer for a phone book. Come prepared. You're more likely to leave with a job.

5.   Inability to express yourself. Sometimes what you know isn't nearly as important as how you articulate. If you have the solution to the world's problems, but can't convey this to anyone, you don't truly have the solution.

6. Not speaking clearly. Don't make the interviewer feel like he or she needs a hearing aide. There is nothing more frustrating than to continually having to ask someone to repeat themselves because they are mumbling.

7.   Lack of experience. Now this is the Catch 22 of job interviews. Often times you can't get hired because you don't have experienced -- and you can't get experience unless you get hired.   However, when you are interviewing you can present yourself in such a way that you convey to your interviewer areas of knowledge or interest which will put you ahead of other applicants.

8.   Inability to explain problem areas. Let's say you were fired from a job. How do you explain this to the interviewer in a way that is positive? Obviously being

fired is not the happiest of occasions -- but what you gained from the experience can be useful to you in the future. What did you learn from the experience? Where have you improved? These are the kinds of things that will impress an interviewer -- even if you are trying to explain a negative occurrence.

9. A sloppy application form. We've talked about it already -- when you are filling out the SF-171 (or any application for that matter) make sure you type it or print very neatly. Remember what we said -- this will be the first impression you make on your potential employer.

10. Failure to let the interviewer know you appreciate his or her time and letting the person who conducted the interview know that you didn't take his or her time for granted.

Under the best of circumstances an interview is nerve-racking and tense. So much rides on how well received you are that it's hard to remain calm.   Just try to keep in mind that even the person doing the interviewing has had to sit in your chair at one time or another. They are not the enemy. It is, however, their job to try to select the best candidate(s) possible to fill a vacancy. How that vacancy is filled can change at the drop of a hat. All you can do is give it your best shot. If you are confident and well prepared you are likely to do much better. Confidence is something that may only come to you after you've gone through a few interviews. Don't let this distress you. Use each interview as a learning tool. There is no 100% right or wrong way. Gear each interview to the situation at hand, and the type of person doing the interviewing. Some people will make you feel more comfortable than others. After you are done make notes about what went well and what didn't. Before long you'll be a pro -- and you'll get the job!

40

7.0 FEDERAL PAY SYSTEMS

Federal employees are covered by several different pay systems. The three major mandated pay systems for federal white collar employees are those for the General Schedule, the Foreign Service, and for certain employees working for the Department of Veterans Affairs.

How difficult an assigned task is and how much responsibility it entails, plus the level of qualification you will need help to determine the classification or grade assigned to a particular federal job. The pay for a particular job is for the assigned grade. In this way the federal government attempts to give equal pay for essentially equal work. The federal government also tries to see that the pay scales for federal employees are comparable to those of the private sector at the same level of difficulty and responsibility. The government usually adjusts salaries and wages each year based on a comparison to private employer salaries.

The largest pay system is the General Schedule (GS). This covers the majority of white collar positions (professional, administrative, technical and clerical) in the Executive Branch -- plus positions within certain agencies of the Legislative and Judicial Branches. The GS consists of 18 grades covering the full range of white collar work. A salary range of ten steps is provided for grades GS-1 through GS-15. There are nine steps for GS-16, five steps for GS-17, and one step for GS-18. Salary rates progress at about 30% within each grade from step 1 through 10.

Advancements within the various grades are scheduled after each 52 weeks of service in steps 1, 2 and 3. Once you reach steps 4, 5 and 6 the advancements are scheduled after 104 weeks of service. Individuals reaching steps 7, 8 and 9 will receive advancements after 156 weeks. To qualify for advancement to the next higher step, an employee must maintain work at an acceptable level of performance. Employees who demonstrate high quality work may advance more rapidly through the rate ranges for their grades by being given additional step increases. These are called *quality step increases*. An employee can only receive one of these types of increases during any 52 week period. It is quite common for an individual to be promoted to a higher grade without having to go through each step on their previous grade.

There are also situations where employees are entitled to what is known as premium pay. This includes pay for overtime; working on holidays, Sundays, or at night; and doing work which involves certain physical hardships or hazards.

Recent college graduates who are hired in professional or administrative positions generally start at either the GS-5 or GS-7 grade level. Graduates with advanced degrees are usually hired into positions at a higher grade level like GS-9 or GS-11. New employees usually get recruited at the step one rate for their grade, with an exception being made for positions authorized in the shortage category. Positions which often fall into the shortage category include engineers, physicists, chemists, metallurgists, astronomers, mathematicians, architects and other technologists.

7.1 VACATION AND SICK LEAVE

Vacation and sick leave allowances are quite liberal in the federal governments' employ. Your vacation days are earned according to the number of years you've been in the federal service. You earn 13 days a year for the first three years, 20 days a year for the next 12, and 26 days a year after 15 years of continued service. You can use all of your leave each year -- or you may accumulate up to six weeks. Part-time employees earn annual leave on a prorated basis.

Thirteen days of seek leave are earned each year. The idea behind these days is to give employees time off for illnesses, medical care and maternity leave. Unlike many, many private sector policies, federal employees can accumulate sick pay without limit and take it when needed. In other words, if you have thirteen days this year, and you are only sick 5 days, next year you will have another thirteen days -- plus the 8 remaining from the previous year for a total of twenty one (21) sick days.

Usually you can transfer both your annual and sick leave from one federal agency to another if you transfer to another federal job. When you leave the federal service you are entitled to a lump sum payment for the amount of annual leave you have earned but have not taken. Take note, this is for your annual leave -- not your sick pay.

The federal government also has a program called the Leave Transfer Program. Under this program federal workers who wish to do so can transfer unused annual leave to colleagues who need the extra paid time off for family or medical emergencies.

Federal employees are currently entitled to 10 paid national holidays each year.

7.2 FEDERAL EMPLOYEES RETIREMENT SYSTEM

The federal government provides an excellent retirement program for its employees designed to give financial security to the employee and his or her family. The Federal Employees Retirement System (FERS), is a three-tiered system designed to be responsive to the changing times and employee needs. Many of its features are portable so that if you leave federal employment, you may still be eligible for benefits.

FERS provides benefits from three different sources: a Basic Benefit Plan, Social Security and the Thrift Savings Plan. Both the employee and the government make contributions each pay period to the Basic Benefit and Social Security parts of FERS. The government puts in a contribution equal to one percent of your pay each pay period into the Thrift Savings plan account that is automatically set up for you when you become a federal employee. Federal employees can also make tax deductible contributions to the savings plan and a portion will be matched by the government.

7.3 HEALTH BENEFITS

Federal employees can choose from a number of health benefit plans under the Federal Employees Health Benefits Program. This choice allows employees flexibility in selecting the kind and amount of insurance protection they actually need and/or want. The government contributes to part of the cost of the premiums.

Group life insurance is provided for all federal employees. Coverage is available on several levels, with optional coverage available for spouses and children. An employee must elect basic life insurance to be eligible for any of the other types of optional programs. The government contributes to part of the cost of the premium for basic insurance, and the employee pays the balance (along with the entire costs for the optional insurance) through payroll deductions.

7.4 WORK SCHEDULES

Numerous options are available for management's consideration in getting a job done and in meeting the needs of a constantly changing and diverse work force. There are full-time, part-time, flexitime or alternate work schedules used in the federal government. Homebound employment is even allowed in some instances.

7.5 TRAINING AND DEVELOPMENT OPPORTUNITIES

Federal employees are given a wide range of opportunities, both formal and informal, for continuation of their education and learning.

These programs cover everything from on-the-job training through formal programs at residential training facilities. The federal government seeks to challenge its employees with training and development programs which will enrich their personal and professional growth.

Each agency's training and development programs are designed to meet a variety of employee training needs, in order to help the government build a core of employees who are up-to-date on scientific, professional, technical and management skills. The types of training provided include:

1. Employee orientation training to familiarize new hires with the mission, objective and operation of the agency for which they will work.

2. Technical skills training and professional education which help employees perform their job better.

3. Supervisory training to increase the ability to manage the work of employees, which includes the ability to delegate and assign work; keep work to specific performance standards; personnel management, and the rights and responsibilities of managers.

4. Executive and management training in areas like national policy and public policy formulation, fundamentals of public administration and administrative theory, resources allocation, leadership and organizational change.

7.6 **TRANSFER POTENTIAL**

Once you're hired by the government, you will have unlimited opportunities to utilize your education and work experience. If you have the desire, you will have the opportunity to advance rapidly in interesting and rewarding career opportunities throughout the U.S. and overseas. A major advantage of working for the government is its ability to offer unmatched opportunities to move from occupation to occupation, from agency to agency, and from one location to another. There is no other employer encompassing this scope or possessing the size to make these types of changes possible.

7.7 **PROMOTION**

Anyone who shows initiative, ability and a willingness to accept greater responsibility will have no trouble at all advancing in the federal service. Advancement opportunities are competitive and are based on performance and merit. Every agency has a Merit Promotion Program which is designed to make sure promotions go to the best qualified employees. Numerous challenging work opportunities exist for individuals with the drive and ambition to advance. Mobility within the federal service can lead to other advancement opportunities which cross organization lines within agencies or by transfer to other agencies.

7.8 **OTHER BENEFITS**

Here are some of the other benefits government employees enjoy:

1. Paid travel and moving expenses to the first post of duty for shortage category occupations.
2. Child care arrangements, credit unions, recreation associations, employee organizations and fitness centers.

3. Diverse and extensive research opportunities with some of the most highly talented and creative people in the United States working in government laboratories.
4. Knowing that you are doing work which is worthwhile and is of service to your country.

8.0 DETAILS ON VETERANS & MILITARY DEPENDENT HIRING PROGRAMS

The federal government has several civil service employment programs aimed at veterans which include **Veterans Preference; Veterans Readjustment Act (VRA);** and for military dependents and spouses of active duty personnel, **Military Spouse Preference Program and the Family Member Preference Program.**

When a vacancy exists within an agency, the selecting official has a number of ways in which he or she can fill the position. These include:

1. Internal promotions or reassignments of existing federal workers.
2. Re-hiring former employees who qualify.
3. Using approved special purpose noncompetitive appointments like the VRA, Spouse Preference, and Military Dependent programs.
4. Bringing in a new employee who has successfully qualified for government employment.

The agency is required to select from the top rated eligible applicants when trying to fill a vacancy. Veterans Preference provides that a veteran may not be passed over for appointment by a non-preference individual who is lower on the list unless there is some compelling reason for doing so.

Veterans are given a **five point** preference if they served on active duty:

1. During war; from April 6, 1917 - July 2, 1921; December 7, 1941 - April 28, 1952; or during the Gulf War.
2. Served in a campaign or expedition for which a campaign badge has been authorized.
3. Served during the period of April 28, 1952 through July 1, 1955.
4. Served for more than 180 consecutive days, any part of which occurred after January 31, 1955 and before October 15, 1976.

Ten point preferences are given to disabled vets who have a **30% rated disability,** and who served on active duty at any time. The disability has to be service connected. Wives, husbands, widows, widowers and mothers of disabled veterans also receive preference in some cases. If you think you qualify for a 10-point preference, review the requirements described in the Standard Form (SF) 15, Application for 10-Point Veteran Preference. The SF 15 is available from any Federal Job Information Center.

Any veteran who has received a Purple Heart is considered to have a service connected disability; as well as compensably disabled (less than 30%); or compensably disabled (30% or more); or spouse, widow(er) or mother of a deceased or disabled veteran.

You cannot receive veteran preference if you are retired or plan to retire at or above the rank of major or lieutenant commander, unless you are disabled.

8.1 HOW DO THE FIVE AND TEN POINT PREFERENCES WORK?

Everyone applying for a federal job is evaluated on their knowledge, skills and abilities on a point system. You will receive points for things like education related to the job you're seeking, experience, special skills, awards and written tests. The maximum number of points anyone can obtain is 100. If you are an eligible five point preference veteran and you have a actual score of 80, five additional points are awarded on preference, giving you a total score of 85. A 10 point preference vet would have a score of 90 in this example. It is not uncommon for individuals to have perfect scores when using the veteran's preference.

Veterans can be given special consideration when applying for vacancies with the government. A veteran can file an application with the OPM **after** an examination has closed. If a current list of eligibles exists, the veteran can apply within 120 days from discharge. Ten point preference veterans **can apply anytime** to be placed on an existing eligibles list.

Announcements which are usually closed to the general public after a specific period of time, can still be available to veterans. All veterans, regardless of when they served on active duty, can file an application for any examination which was open while he or she was in the armed forces or which was announced within 120 days after his or her separation if the veteran makes application within 120 days after receiving an **honorable discharge.**

Disabled veterans receive 10 points preference and are able to file an application at any time for any position for which there is a list of eligibles, or for which a list is about to be established, or for which a non-temporary appointment has been made in the preceding three years.

If you or a family member are interested in receiving more information about this point system, you can obtain a Veterans Preference brochure called *"Veterans' Preference in Federal Employment".* from the U.S. Office of Personnel Management, Work force Effectiveness and Development Group, Office of Affirmative Employment Programs, Washington, D.C. 20415. There is no charge for this booklet.

About 30% of our government employees are veterans. The average salary is over $30,000 a year, and many veterans are able to begin employment with 4 weeks of vacation per year because military time counts toward their federal benefits.

8.2 VETERAN READJUSTMENT APPOINTMENTS (VRA's)

VRA appointments used to be confined strictly to Vietnam Era Veterans. However, Public Law 101-237 expanded VRA appointments to include hundreds of thousands of Post Vietnam Era Veterans. This change may mean that you are eligible for a non-competitive federal government job appointment. The VRA has been extended through December 31, 1993. here are some of the highlights of the new law:

1. Time limits have been changed to a four year period after discharge; or a two year period after the President signed the bill into law on December 18, 1989.
2. The education restrictions have been altered from no more than 14 years of education to no more than 16 years, unless the individual is a veteran receiving disability compensation.
3. Provides for a four year extension through December of 1993.
4. The eligibility has been changed to "certain Vietnam era veterans and post-Vietnam era veterans". In other words, Vietnam era veterans are eligible if they have a service connected disability; or if during such era served on active duty in the Armed Forces in a campaign or expedition for which a campaign badge has been authorized; and a veteran who served on active duty after the Vietnam era.

This is quite a change from previous law. In the past the law gave only Vietnam era veterans the opportunity to be appointed non-competitively to any federal agency. Now all veterans who served on active duty after the Vietnam era (1975 on) are eligible for direct non-competitive appointments.

A VRA appointment means that a veteran can be hired by any federal agency without having to go through the Office of Personnel Management. An agency that has a vacancy can hire a VRA candidate immediately. This is much quicker than the six months it often takes if the agency has to go through OPM.

VRA appointments are for two years. If the VRA employee performs satisfactorily during that time period her or she must be given a career appointment. In other words, if you do your work well and complete all of the training requirements at the end of two years you will have a full time government job.

VRA appointees can be hired at grades up to a GS-11 ($32,423), depending upon their status, experience, background and the position for which they have applied.

You can apply for the VRA program by completing an SF-171 application form and sending it to agencies for which you wish to work. Be sure to submit a cover letter with your application which explains that you are a VRA candidate and would like to be considered for an appointment with that agency. The employer has the ability to hire you directly, if they like what they see on your application.

After you've given the agency time to review your application, make sure you follow up with a phone call. You may even want to call the agency prior to sending your SF-171 to find out whose attention you need to send it to. Send your application to every department that interests you! Just make sure you remember that each SF-171 has to be personally signed.

An agency doesn't have to hire through the VRA program, so don't expect miracles if your skills aren't suitable for a particular job. Only if your education and work experience meet the needs of a department or agency will you be considered.

8.2.1 Eligibility

You must be a veteran who (1) served on active duty for a period of more than 180 days and was discharged or released thereafter with other than a dishonorable discharge, or (2) was discharged or released from active duty because of a service related disability.

There is a time limit on eligibility which is the four year (4) period beginning on the date of the veteran's last discharge or release from active duty, or the two year (2) period beginning on the date of the enactment of the law, whichever is later.

You must have been discharged within the four (4) years preceding the expiration date of the current law, which is December 31, 1993. After December 17, 1991 almost no Vietnam era vets will be eligible for a VRA unless he or she has recently been discharged or is retiring.

8.2.2 Authorized Campaign Badge for Vietnam Era Service

You need to show documentation of a Vietnam veteran's eligibility for an authorized campaign badge on the Form DD-214, Certificate of Release from Active Duty. More information about campaign badges and expeditionary medals authorized for operations during the Vietnam era can be found in the Federal Personnel Manual Supplement 296-33, Subchapter 7.

The Department of Defense (DOD) has established the dates of service medals and campaign badges. The Vietnam Service Medal is authorized from July 3, 1965 to March 28, 1973. The Vietnam era runs from August 5, 1964 to May 7, 1975.

8.3 MILITARY DEPENDENT HIRING PROGRAMS

As we have mentioned, dependents of military and civilian sponsors and spouses of active duty military personnel receive hiring preference when they apply for civilian employment with Department of Defense agencies. The Military Family Act of 1985 expanded hiring preference to many jobs previously not available to this program and for jobs within the States, Territories and U.S. Possessions.

In the past, the U.S. Army in Europe has hired over 100,000 civilian employees. Obviously with Defense Budget cuts not being put into effect, these numbers will be altered, but there are still opportunities available.

Family Member Employment Assistance Programs are available at most large bases. These programs are sponsored by local Civilian Employment Offices, and Family Support Centers to provide employment information, career assistance and counseling. Additionally they provide job skills training and personal development workshops.

8.3.1 The Military Spouse Preference Program

This program concentrates on placing husbands or wives of military personnel into competitive civil service vacancies across the U.S., our Territories, Possessions, foreign areas and the District of Columbia. Noncompetitive positions for Spouse Preference are usually Excepted Service and Nonappropriated Fund Instrumentality (NAFI) positions. NAFI jobs are in service clubs, exchanges, retail stores, snack bars, base service and related activities.

Preference is also given for DOD civilian positions for which a military spouse is best qualified at pay grades GS-1 through GS-15 or the equivalent. The term best qualified doesn't mean the highest rated candidate. In this instance the term means anyone who meets the basic requirements for a particular job. Most often the only candidates with a higher preference are veterans and career civil service employees who have been displaced from their jobs through a reduction in armed forces.

8.3.2 Excepted Service and NAFI Positions

Most overseas positions are Excepted Service and do not require OPM eligibility. (See Section 2.4) Each employing CPO maintains a list of qualified and available candidates. Excepted Service applicants must complete an SF-171 application and supplemental forms required by the CPO. Applicants for NAFI positions require a service application form such as the Army's DA-3433. Any forms necessary will be provided by the local CPO.

8.3.3 Eligibility

A spouses' eligibility starts 30 days before his or her military sponsor's overseas reporting date. A spouse who has less than six months time remaining in an area may be non-selected for any permanent full-time positions since they won't be there long enough to provide the service needed. Preference entitlement ends when the spouse accepts or declines any position expected to last longer than 12 months at any acceptable grade level. Preference is limited to openings in the same commuting area as that of the new duty station. A spouse wishing to take a position outside the commuting area may do so, but will not receive preference. A spousal preference can be used ONLY ONCE for each permanent relocation of the military member.

Spouses can apply for preference at any armed forces or defense agency facility within the commuting area of the military member's duty station. Applications can be submitted at any service branch in the general area. The local CPO has information outlining employment opportunities and application forms.

The National Security Agency and Defense Intelligence Agencies do not participate in spouse and family member preference programs.

8.3.4. Family Member Preference

The majority of family member positions are clerical in nature. Family members can apply for any position for which they are qualified though. Family members of both military and civilian sponsors are given equal preference for positions designated for U.S. citizen occupancy, after military spouse and veteran's preference, for employment in non-supervisory positions at pay grades of GS-8 or below.

Usually, family members are appointed under excepted appointments which cannot extend longer than two months beyond the sponsor's departure or separation date. Family members who have been hired under this program don't acquire competitive civil service status, but may gain eligibility for Federal Civil Service re-employment when they return to the States under Executive Order 12362.

Army, Air Force, Navy and Marine installation Family Support Centers work with local CPOs to offer family members employment assistance, career counseling, and in some cases, training to advance skill levels. Family Support Centers have slightly different names within each military branch. In the Army they are called

Army Community service offices. You can contact your local Support Center for more information.

If a military sponsor is being relocated to a new duty station, family members should contact the CPO or Family Support Center at the new location to request information regarding employment.

Spouse preference applicants must submit an SF-171 employment application along with a detailed statement. The statement needs to include:

1) Your name
2) The name of the installation or activity at which are making application
3) A statement that you have not been offered and declined a position for which you applied under spousal preference during your current PCS
4) The position title or number for which you are applying.
5) A copy of the service member's official orders need to be attached to your statement.

9.0 EMPLOYMENT OPPORTUNITIES OVERSEAS

Thousands of Americans work for the federal government in foreign countries, in the U.S. territories, Alaska and Hawaii. The jobs most commonly filled are administrative (technical and professional), accountants, auditors, budget and program officers, management analysts, nurses, procurement officers, shorthand reporters, equipment specialists, engineers, social workers, housing officers, teachers, and alcohol and drug abuse specialists. Unfortunately, most clerical positions are usually filled by local people overseas.

These jobs are filled in a number of ways. In the U.S. territories, Hawaii and Alaska most jobs are filled through competitive civil service announcements. Some positions overseas are filled through Excepted Service and Non appropriated Fun Instrumentality (NAFI) hiring programs.

When vacancies are filled locally overseas, U.S. citizens living abroad, dependents of citizens employed or stationed overseas, or foreign nationals can be hired. Most countries have agreements with the United States which require the hiring of local nationals whenever possible to help the local economy. All positions held by foreign nationals are in the Excepted Service. Excepted Service jobs are no subject to the OPM's competitive hiring requirements.

9.1 JOBS IN THE PACIFIC REGIONS

There are federal civil service employees in Hawaii, Guam, Japan, Korea, the Philippines, and American Samoa. Most federal jobs in the Pacific overseas areas are with the Department of Defense. While military spending cutbacks are affecting the number of jobs available, there are still positions which need to be filled. Many positions in DOD agencies are presently filled under a special appointment authority for hiring family members of U.S. military or civilian personnel stationed in foreign areas. Jobs not filled by the special appointment authority are often filled by federal employees transferring overseas or by U.S. citizens living in the local areas on a temporary or short term basis. The greatest demand is for experienced engineering, administrative, educational, technical or scientific occupations.

Federal employees living in Hawaii and Guam are given a cost-of-living allowance (COLA) in addition to their basic pay. The COLA is 22.5% on Oahu, 17.5% on Kauai, 20% on Maui, Lanai and Molokai, and 15% on Hawaii. Other Pacific areas pay COLA ranging from 10 to 20% above standard pay.

For information about temporary job vacancies and recruitment for shortage category positions you can contact the following:

FJIC
Federal Building, Room 5316
300 Ala Moana Blvd.
Honolulu, HI 96850

FJIC and Testing Center
Pacific News Building, Rm 902
238 Archbishop Flores St.
Agana, Guam 96910

Industrial Relations Office
Pearl Harbor Naval Shipyard, Box 400
Pearl Harbor, HI 96860-5352

Central Personnel Office
15th Air Base Wing (DPCS)
Hickam AFB, HI 96853

Consolidated CPO (Navy)
Guam 33, Box 183, U.S. Naval Stn.
FPO San Francisco, CA 96630

U.S. Army CPO, Hawaii
Bldg. T-1500 (Attn: APZV-CPR)
Fort Shafter, HI 96858-5000

Consolidated CPO (Navy)
4300 Radford Drive
Honolulu, HI 96818-3298

Civilian Personnel Office
43 Combat Support Group
APO San Francisco, CA 96334

9.2 **OPPORTUNITIES IN THE ATLANTIC**

Most of these positions are in Germany, Belgium, Italy and Africa. Most of these jobs are filled by residents of the host country or by family members of military or civilian personnel stationed in Europe. Approximately 5% are U.S. citizens who have been recruited outside of Europe.

USAREUR (U.S. ARMY EUROPE) publishes a booklet titled "Jobs In Europe" which explains status and nonstatus applicants. This booklet gives a listing of jobs for which USAREUR is accepting applications, as well as giving you the minimum qualification requirements for vacancies. The booklet is updated several times each year and can be obtained by writing to:

U.S. Army, Europe & Seventh Army
Civilian Recruitment Center
Attn: AEAGA-CRC
APO, NY 09403-0101

9.3 **THINGS YOU NEED TO KNOW ABOUT FOREIGN JOBS**

Individuals who are hired to work overseas must meet various requirements which may differ a bit from what would be expected for a job in the continental U.S.

Prior to being accepted for an overseas position you will be required to pass a thorough physical exam. In many cases, any dependents who will be accompanying you will also be required to pass a physical exam. You must be able to physically adapt to the conditions at various locations which may not have adequate health care available. Individuals taking medications or who require special care will not be considered for some positions. Any physical impairment which would create a hazard to yourself or others, or would reduce your level of performance on a job will disqualify you.

ALL applicants considered for appointment to an overseas position must pass a comprehensive security clearance, plus a character and suitability check. These investigations can take quite a while to complete, so you are appointed conditionally pending the results.

If hired, you will be required to sign a transportation agreement which typically states your tour will last from twelve to thirty six months.

You may find that a foreign language that would not be a requirement for a position in the States may be required for some overseas jobs. The job announcement will specify if a language is required. Many agencies hire candidates without the required language skills and then give them a period of time to develop acceptable proficiency.

Most agencies allow professional employees to take their dependents along. Professional positions are usually considered to be mid-level and above. Other employees can usually arrange for dependents to follow them at a later date.

The pay for overseas positions is usually the same as that received state side. There may be additional allowances such as post differential, cost-of-living and quarters allowance when conditions call for them. Military base privileges are authorized in many instances. Department of Defense schools are available for dependent children through the 12th grade.

Since there are relatively few overseas opportunities, the competition is quite fierce. If you are well qualified in an occupation and are available to travel to just about any location, your chances of getting selected are good. Because of the rotation of current employees back to the U.S., there are usually a number of new jobs.

You can only apply for overseas employment with our government if you are a U.S. citizen or an American Samoan. Make sure you apply well ahead of when you will actually be available for work. Applications generally take between six and eight weeks just to process. Many jobs limit the number of applications available and the time allowed for filing. Applications are given out until the limit is reached or until the closing date of the vacancy.

Federal agencies hire lots of temporary employees. You may be considered for both temporary and permanent positions. If you take a temporary job, your name will still remain on the register for consideration for a permanent position. Temporary jobs usually last for a year or less, but in some instances they last up to four years.

For individuals truly wishing for the experience of working in a foreign country, our government is one of your best bets! Jobs in the private sector do exist, but they are most often filled from within the structure of a company by someone who has "paid their dues". Additionally, working for the government in a foreign country will give you a built in support system you wouldn't have with a private company. Many of the people with whom you would be working are also from the United States.

10.0 DOING WHAT IT TAKES TO GET THE JOB

If you are really serious about working for the government, you have a leg up on your competition. Many, many people begin the application process only to drop out along the way because they get frustrated by the amount of paperwork necessary, or the delays in finding a job. If you are willing to commit yourself to this job search and will thoroughly complete each application necessary -- and actively pursue all job vacancies for which you are qualified -- nothing will stop you.

Anyone interested in working for the government should start researching the system, familiarizing themselves with the various jobs available, preparing for any tests they may be required to take months before they expect to actually be hired.

Many people seeking work make the mistake of sending in only one application for an announcement they see. If you are serious about finding work, you will send applications to EVERY job for which you are qualified. Remember, the idea is to get hired. Once you are a part of the system, you can transfer into an agency or department you desire.

Contact numerous FJIC's to request bids. In this way you will find out how you are rated. Then you can send copies of your rating notification and SF-171 to agencies for which you would consider working. ALWAYS send a short cover letter explaining what job you are interested in. Give them some personal background information on you in the letter too.

If you are willing to relocate, you also have an advantage over many applicants. Even in today's depressed economy and scarce job market, there are lots of people who are either unwilling or unable to move. Don't be one of them! There are many excellent jobs with various governmental agencies which require you to live in a not so wonderful location. Again, get your foot in the door. Once you've obtained the required experience and training, you will be able to transfer to a better location. And who knows, you may find that a location someone else finds less than desirable will feel like home to you!

It's important to remember that your first move will be at your expense. If you are willing to relocate, you will be responsible for the cost of the move. However, if you bid out to another location after your first year of employment the government will pick up the tab. Their moving allowances are generous. It is not unheard of for an agency to buy your house from you at market rates, pay for the move and pay real estate sales commissions and closing costs at your new location. But wait, there's more -- you will also receive 60 days temporary quarters expenses at your new location and a free house hunting trip may even be part of the deal.

One word of advice: While you may be able to find a job by taking an employment offer in a place less than desirable, you'll want to make sure you can afford to live where you are considering taking a job. Many agencies have a very difficult time filling jobs in high cost areas like New York, Los Angeles and Washington, D.C. Make sure you have a clear understanding of the cost of living in the area you are thinking about before you jump at an offer.

Don't let rejection turn you off to government employment. You are bound to apply for jobs that don't result in a hire. Learn from these rejections. You have every right to contact the selecting official. Talk to them to see what held you back. If you need more training, ask them how you can obtain it. Maybe you simply failed to convey the skills you possess in a way that convinced them to hire you. While you don't want to spend time arguing with the person who did the selection, you can learn valuable information from them which will help you obtain a future job. Take their advice and revise your application for the next vacancy. You should even send the selecting official a thank you note for their consideration with a revised application which incorporates the changes they suggested. Ask them to keep your revised SF-171 for future consideration.

Make sure you begin networking so that you keep contact with each and every government employee who crosses your path. People who are already working for the government will be highly valuable to you in your job search. If they learn to trust and respect you, they'll be likely to let you know about potential openings -- often before the general public.

Once you've finished reviewing this book, your next step should be to start contacting as many government agencies as possible to see what they have available. Our supplementary job listing will also provide you with valuable information you can use to make contacts. If you see a job that particularly interests you , look it up in our job description section. This section will give you a brief overview of what an actual job entails. Again, the more familiar you are with how the government works, the better your chances of finding work.

Postal jobs have not been outlined or explained in this directory, but this is another area in which you may wish to look. If you are interested in obtaining work with the post office you should take a look at our "HOW TO GET A UNITED STATES POSTAL SERVICE JOB". This directory provides a great overview of how to seek employment, providing valuable samples of test questions and other information which will assist you in your job search.

11.0 STATE AND LOCAL GOVERNMENT JOBS

State and local (city and county) governments provide a large and expanding source of job opportunities in a wide variety of occupational fields. Some 80,000 state and local government agencies employ over 13.5 million people; nearly three-fourths of these people work in units of local government such as counties, municipalities, towns and school districts. New job opportunities from retirement and deaths alone result in the need for more than 100,000 new workers annually.

Educational services account for about one-half of all jobs in state and local government. Almost 7 million government employees work in public schools, college or other educational services. In addition to more than 3.6 million instructional personnel, school systems, college and universities also employ almost 2.9 million administrative personnel, librarians, guidance counselors, nurses, dieticians, clerks and maintenance workers. Three-fourths of these work in elementary and secondary schools, which are administered by local governments. State employment in education is concentrated chiefly at the college, university and technical school levels.

The next largest field of state and local government employment is health services. The 1.5 million workers employed in health and hospital work include physicians, nurses, medical laboratory technicians and hospital attendants.

General governmental control and financial activities account for about 800,000 workers. These include chief executives and their staffs, legislative representatives and persons employed in the administration of justice, tax enforcement and other financial work, and general administration. These functions require the services of individuals such as lawyers, judges and other court officials, city managers, property assessors, budget analysts, stenographers and clerks.

More than 560,000 people work in street and highway construction and maintenance. Highway workers include civil engineers, surveyors, operators of construction machinery and equipment, truck drivers, concrete finishers, carpenters, toll collectors and construction laborers.

Police and fire protection is another large field of employment. More than 620,000 persons are engaged in police work, including administrative, clerical and custodial personnel, as well as uniformed and plainclothes police. Local governments employ all of the 270,000 fire protection employees, as well as most of the police. One out of five firefighters is employed part time.

Other state and local government employees work in a wide variety of activities: Local utilities (such as water or electricity), transportation, natural resources, public welfare, parks and recreation, sanitation, corrections, local libraries, sewage disposal, and housing and urban renewal. These activities require workers in diverse occupations such as economists, electrical engineers, electricians, pipefitters, clerks, foresters and bus drivers.

Clerical, administrative, maintenance and custodial work make up a large portion of employment in most government agencies. Among the workers involved in these activities are clerk-typists, stenographers, secretaries, office managers, fiscal and budget administrators, bookkeepers, accountants, carpenters, painters, plumbers, guards and janitors.

11.1 **EMPLOYMENT TRENDS AND OUTLOOK**

The long-range trend in state and local government employment has been steadily upward. Much of this growth has resulted from the need to provide additional services as population increases and as people move from rural to urban areas. City development has required additional street and highway facilities, schools, police and fire protection and public health, sanitation, welfare and other services. Population growth and increasing personal income have generated demand for additional and improved education, housing, health facilities and other services. Except for education, needs for these government services are expected to increase through the 1990's. Growth of state and local government is expected to be concentrated in areas other than education. Although state and local government employment is expected to increase more slowly through the 1990's, large numbers of workers will be needed to replace employees who transfer to other fields of work, retire, or die.

Most, though by no means all, positions in state and local government are filled by residents of the state or locality. If shortages of particular skills exist, however, it is often necessary to recruit from outside the area.

11.2 **EARNINGS**

Earnings of state and local government employees vary widely, depending upon occupation and locality. Salary differences from state to state tend to reflect differences in the general wage level in various localities. Salary information can be obtained from the appropriate state and local government agencies and frequently compares **very favorably** with private sector employment opportunities.

A majority of state and local government positions are filled through some type of formal civil service test; that is, personnel are hired and promoted on the basis of merit. In some areas, groups of employees, such as teachers and police, have separate civil service coverage for their specific groups.

Most state and local government employees are covered by retirement systems or by the federal Social Security program. They usually work a standard week of 40 hours or less, with overtime pay or compensatory time benefits for additional hours of work.

11.3   HOW TO FIND & APPLY FOR STATE & LOCAL JOBS

State and local government jobs are filled in several ways:

(A)   Job openings are **advertised directly by the agency** using its own personnel office, newspaper, etc.

(B)   The agency can ask the **State Job Service** to provide it with suitable applicants.

(C)   The agency can ask the **State Department of Personnel** for its recommendations.

(D)   The vacancy can be filled through the **promotion of current employees.**

Let's look more closely at items (A), (B) and (C):

(A)   **State Agencies**

If an agency has advertised its own vacancy, you should send your application directly to that agency. Their doors are almost always open to accept your application and, on many occasions, jobs are not advertised via the State Job Center or Department of Personnel. To pursue this avenue, call, write or visit any of the literally dozens of state agencies you might be interested in working for. Consult your local telephone book under **STATE GOVERNMENT** and drop by your local library and review their copy of the phone book for your state capitol. Here is a partial list of typical state agencies for you to consider.

Air Pollution Control	Nuclear Energy
Attorney General	Occupational Safety
Audit	Parks
Corrections	Fish & Game
Data Processing	Food & Drugs
Drug Abuse	Highway Safety
Economics Development	Prisons
Education (all levels)	Public Works

Elections
Energy
Environment Affairs
Fed & State Relations
Child Welfare
Community Affairs
Consumer Affairs
Historic Preservation
Housing
Human Rights
Juvenile Delinquency
Law Enforcement
Mass Transit

Purchasing
Secretary of State
Social Services
Surplus Property
Taxation & Revenue
Tourism
Treasurer
Veterans Affairs
Water Pollution Ctrl
Weights & Measures
Welfare
Worker's Comp.

Next, you'll need names and addresses for the individual agencies. Remember to **personalize** all requests for job application forms. Call the agency to find out the name of their personnel manager; or if you prefer, call the number of the State Government Information Center. Remember, these office can provide you with lots of useful information but are not connected directly with employment opportunities.

When writing for your job application form, don't forget to enclose a copy of your resume together with a brief cover letter. An example of your cover letter might be as follows:

your street address
city, state, zip
current date

Name of Personnel Manager
Street address
City, state, zip

Dear _____:

    I am interested in working for your agency and would appreciate receiving the necessary job application forms.

    I am enclosing a copy of my resume for your review which indicated my experience in the following areas:

_____.

    I look forward to hearing from you.

                        Very truly yours,

                        Your Name

County and City Agencies

    Hiring for your local city and county is done by the supervisors, managers and directors of the agencies themselves. The Personnel Office for your City or County are typically located in City Hall and County Offices, respectively. Many of these office have job hotlines (recording that tell you which jobs are presently open for applications); these are a valuable time-saver for job hunters, and you should make use of them whenever possible.

    To decide which agencies you would like to work for, again pick up your local phone book and look under **City** or **County Government** for a listing of the agencies. Remember, there is a wide range of jobs continually available in <u>all</u> areas; if you stop and think of all the services provided in your town or city, you'll probably generate a list something like this:

Airports	Libraries
Ambulance Services	Local Elections
Animal Control	Municipal Parking
Audit & Finance	Museums, Zoos, and Golf Courses
Building & Inspections	Parks & Recreation
City Clerk's Office	Public Schools & Ed.
Cultural & Social Services	Public Health
Construction	Public Transit
Engineering	Public Utilities
Fire Protection	Road Construction
Garbage Collection	Sewage Disposal
Harbors	Tourism
Hospitals	Traffic Control
Housing	Welfare/Human Services
Landlord & Tenant Affairs	

ONE NOTE regarding this direct-to-agency application process: when checking with city and county government offices, we found that some DO NOT appreciate applicants initially approaching the individual agencies. To avoid any problems, you should make a single phone call FIRST to the city or county employment office or personnel office to ask them if it is okay if you contact the specific agencies you would like to work for. If they don't mind, they will readily tell you, and you may proceed with contacting the agencies.

Other less obvious sources of job listings which you should be aware of include:

* City Clerk's Office -- call them to see if they have information about current City Department job openings

* Local School Boards -- visit them and file applications. Remember, we're not just talking about teaching positions, but all the support facilities including janitors, maintenance of grounds, engineers, etc.

* Local Newspapers -- occasionally there will be ads in the classified section under "HELP WANTED"

And last, but by no means least, **always** think of friends or acquaintances who may be able to give you a hot tip. If this friend has a government job, keep in very close touch and make a point of frequently checking to see if he/she knows of any new job openings.

Your first step toward getting your job will probably be to call or write and request the particular agency to send you an application form. **(Always try to use the telephone whenever possible. Once you have perfected a courteous, straightforward technique, your perseverance can save enormous amounts of time, especially when it is critical to get information about a particular job quickly. As a rule, you will find people to be extremely helpful, and talking to them in perso**n is more immediate and satisfying than a letter.) Each agency has a somewhat different form; however, content will be very similar and once you have completed one, you'll have no trouble adapting it for other agencies. You'll also want to enclose a copy of your resume with the completed application form.

(B)   <u>State Job Service</u>

A listing of addresses and telephone numbers of the MAIN offices of these State Job Service Centers is listed in Appendix   (page   ) For information on the field offices covering your area, look in the white pages of your local telephone book under "State Government Offices" -- Employment Development Department: **Job Service.**

This agency is usually the largest single employment agency in the state. Not only can they refer you to state and local government job openings, but they also maintain large listings of openings with private companies.

The Job Service employs counselors who are there to review your background and skills (sometimes a test will be administered) and advise you about what you are best qualified to do. Then they will have you check the **Job Book** (a book or microfiche system which has a massive listing of job openings which is updated every day) for current openings for which you qualify; many times they can set up a job interview for you on the spot. **Do be aware** of the fact that the Job Service does NOT deal exclusively with government jobs, so if you want to work for your sate, county or city, <u>you must specify this to your counselor.</u>

Do not forget that special employment services and preferences have been developed for veterans, handicapped and youth. The law requires that veterans be assigned priority in interviewing, counseling, testing and job placement. Disabled veterans are covered by extensive outreach programs in each state. The youth programs placed more than 750,000 youths in summer jobs with state and local government agencies last year!

(C) **State Department of Personnel**

State Department of Personnel offices are maintained in most urban centers, and will be listed in the phone book under "State Government Offices -- Personnel Department." If not available contact your state main office listed in Appendix 5 (page 129).

In contrast to the State Job Service, the State Personnel Office does deal exclusively with **state government** jobs; therefore, if you contact the Personnel Office, you will receive information regarding job openings for state government agencies ONLY. Besides the direct-to-agency method we described above, it's a very good idea to contact the State Personnel Department for their complete listing, as there may be openings for agencies you never even though of or they may have a more updated list for you.

Check ALL avenues; there is so much information out there available to help you get the job you want. And by simultaneously following up several opportunities, you'll get the job you want that much faster.

One last note: we hear occasionally from our customers that their state has imposed a hiring freeze and they are not taking applications. One reader told us his state had not hired anyone for **three years!** It's highly unlikely that in all the state agencies for any one sate **no one** died, **no one** retired, **no one** was promoted, **no one** got fired, and **no one** left to have a baby or take a private job in 3 years! Right? So if you are told there is a hiring freeze in your state, **ASK:** (1) where do they get employees to replace those who die, retire, get fired or leave? and (2) where can you put your name on a list to be considered at the earliest possible time? (3) when is the freeze anticipated to be over? Remember: those who (politely) persevere get more answers than those who just accept the first thing they hear! Again, here is where using the telephone can help you to shortcut your way over obstacles which will discourage your competition!

12.0 GOVERNMENT AGENCY PERSONNEL DEPARTMENTS YOU CAN CONTACT

You've got your work cut out for you right now. You can contact the nearest Office of Personnel Management (OPM), Federal Job Information Center (FJIC), Chief Petty Officer (CPO), agencies outside the competitive system -- and last, but certainly not least -- there is nothing to prevent you from communicating directly with the personnel departments of agencies for which you wish to work. The following is a list of these personnel offices with a brief description of the work they oversee.

AGRICULTURAL RESEARCH SERVICE
PERSONNEL DIVISION
6303 IVY LANE, ROOM 820
GREENBELT, MD 20770

The Agricultural Research Service (ARS) is responsible for planning, developing and implementing research that provides new knowledge and technologies to ensure an adequate supply of food and fiber for the nation's population now and in the future. The Agency's goals and objectives include research and development in the area of natural resources, crop and animal quality and productivity, commodity conversion and delivery, human health and nutrition and scientific information systems. The ARS is the principal scientific research agency of the U.S. Department of Agriculture.

FARMERS HOME ADMINISTRATION
HUMAN RESOURCES
14TH & INDEPENDENCE AVE., SW
WASHINGTON, DC 20250

The Farmers Home Administration provides financial assistance to rural people and communities that cannot obtain commercial credit at affordable terms. The agency encourages and supports family farm ownership and operation; provides financing for adequate individual homes and rental apartments; provides financial assistance for needed community facilities such as streets, health services and recreation centers; provides economic support to farmers affected by disaster and fosters economic development in rural areas.

OFFICE OF PUBLIC AFFAIRS
OFFICE OF PERSONNEL
ROOM 31W, ADMINISTRATION BUILDING
WASHINGTON DC 20250

The Office of Governmental and Public Affairs provides policy direction, review, and coordination of all information programs of the Department. The Office is assigned responsibility for maintaining the flow of information and providing liaison between the Department of Agriculture and the Congress, the mass communication media, State and local governments, and the public.

OFFICE OF THE GENERAL COUNSEL
OFFICE OF PERSONNEL
ROOM 31W, ADMINISTRATION BUILDING
WASHINGTON DC 20250

The General Counsel is the principal legal advisor to the Secretary and is responsible for providing all legal advice and representation in the Department.

RURAL ELECTRIFICATION ADMINISTRATION
PERS MGT DIV, ROOM 4031, SOUTH BLDG
14TH AND INDEPENDENCE AVE, SW
WASHINGTON, DC 20250

The Rural Electrification Administration (REA) was created in 1935 to furnish financial, technical and managerial assistance to rural electric utility borrowers throughout the United States. In 1949, the Rural Electrification Act was amended to include a telephone loan program. The main purpose of the telephone program is to provide low-interest financing as well as technical guidance to rural telephone borrowers. Since its inception, REA's electric and telephone programs have provided assistance to more than 1,000 rural electric and more than 900 rural telephone utility systems in 47 states. As a result of REA's assistance, electric and telephone service is available to more than 96 percent of the nation's farmers. Today, REA continues to make and to guarantee loans to borrowers while exploring ways to improve electric and telephone service to meet increasing and diversifying consumer needs.

NATIONAL AGRICULTURAL RESEARCH SERVICE
PERSONNEL DIVISION
6303 IVY LANE, ROOM 820
GREENBELT, MD 20770

The Agricultural Research Service (ARS) is responsible for planning, developing and implementing research that provides new knowledge and technologies to ensure an adequate supply of food and fiber for the nation's population now and in the future. The Agency's goals and objectives include research and development in the area of natural resources, crop and animal quality and productivity, commodity conversion and delivery, human health and nutrition and scientific information systems. The ARS is the principal scientific research agency of the U.S. Department of Agriculture.

ECONOMIC ANALYSIS STAFF
C/O ECONOMICS MANAGEMENT STAFF
PERSONNEL DIVISION, ROOM 1415, SO. BLDG.
WASHINGTON, DC 20250

The Economic Analysis Staff assists in developing, organizing, coordinating, and synthesizing economic and statistical analyses to be used as a basis for planning and evaluating short-and intermediate-range agricultural policy. The Staff also develops economic and statistical analyses to evaluate complex interagency domestic and foreign agricultural problems and issues. The Staff reviews and evaluates recommendations submitted by USDA agencies, task forces, and study groups for their impact upon the agricultural economy. It analyzes the economic policy implications of legislative proposals of the Department and of Congress. The Staff also represents the Department in meetings with agriculture, industry, and consumer groups to discuss the economic impact of existing and proposed Department policies.

NATIONAL AGRICULTURAL STATISTICS
C/O ECONOMICS MANAGEMENT STAFF
PERSONNEL DIV, ROOM 1415, SO. BLDG.
WASHINGTON, DC 20250

The National Agricultural Statistics Service (NASS) prepares estimates and reports on production, supply, price,and other items necessary for the orderly operation of the U.S. agricultural economy. NASS prepares these estimates through a complex system of sample surveys of producers, processors, buyers, and others associated with agriculture. Information is gathered by mail, telephone, personal interviews and field visits. The 44 State-Federal offices, serving all 50 States, and the national office prepare weekly, monthly, annual, and other periodic reports for free distribution to the news media, Congress, and survey respondents. The reports are available to others on a subscription basis. Data on crop and livestock products appears in over 300 reports issued annually. Cooperative agreements with State agencies also permit preparation and publication of estimates of individual crops and livestock by counties in most States.

OFFICE OF THE INSPECTOR GENERAL
OFFICE OF PERSONNEL, ROOM 31-W
ADMINISTRATION BUILDING
WASHINGTON, DC   20250

Thousands of indictments and convictions, millions of dollars in restitutions and fines, millions more dollars identified to be recovered and numerous management improvements are the legacies left by the Office of the Inspector General (OIG) for its work over the past 25 years. OIG has had highly talented, imaginative employees throughout its history. Over the years, it has met the challenge of vastly expanded USDA budgets and programs by providing its people with training and skills on the cutting edge of advanced audit and investigative techniques, not the least of which is the extensive use of computers.   OIG is responsible for leadership and coordination in promoting economy, efficiency and effectiveness, and detecting and preventing fraud, waste and abuse in USDA's programs and operations. To carry out its responsibilities, OIG conducts and supervises audits and investigations and keeps agency officials and the Congress informed about problems and deficiencies in the administration of the programs and operations and about the necessity for and progress of corrective action.

OFFICE OF ENERGY
C/O ECONOMICS MANAGEMENT STAFF
PERSONNEL DIVISION, ROOM 1415, SO. BLDG.
WASHINGTON, DC 20250

The Office of Energy serves as the focal point for all energy-related matters within the Department. The Office is responsible for developing and coordinating all USDA energy policies, reviewing and evaluating all USDA energy and energy-related programs, and providing liaison with the Department of Energy and other Federal agencies and departments on energy activities that may affect agriculture and rural America. The Office also represents the Department in meetings with agriculture, industry, and consumer groups to discuss impacts of departmental energy policies, programs, and proposals.

ECONOMIC MANAGEMENT STAFF
PERSONNEL DIVISION
ROOM 1415, SOUTH BUILDING
WASHINGTON DC 20250

The Economics Management Staff provides management services to the National Agricultural Statistics Service, the Economic Research Service, the World Agricultural Outlook Board, the Economic Analysis Staff, and the Office of Energy. These services include budget, financial management, personnel and related programs, administrative services, information, equal opportunity and civil rights, and general management assistance.

FOOD SAFETY AND INSPECTION SERVICE
PERS DIV, ROOM 3143, SOUTH BUILDING
14TH AND INDEPENDENCE AVENUE, SW
WASHINGTON, DC 20250

The mission of the Food Safety and Inspection Service (FSIS) is to insure that the nation's commercial supply of meat and poultry products is safe, wholesome and correctly labeled and packaged. FSIS provides plant inspection of all domestic establishments preparing meat or poultry products for sale or distribution in commerce; reviews foreign inspection systems and establishments that prepare meat or poultry products for export to the United States and provides assistance to states that maintain meat and poultry inspection programs. The Agency tests meat and poultry products for the presence of unlawful drugs, chemical residues and other adulterants. FSIS also monitors food distribution channels to prevent violations of meat and poultry inspection laws.

WORLD AGRICULTURAL OUTLOOK BOARD
C/O ECONOMICS MANAGEMENT STAFF
PERSONNEL DIVISION, ROOM 1415, SO. BLDG.
WASHINGTON DC 20250

The World Agricultural Outlook Board coordinates and reviews all commodity and aggregate agricultural and food data and analyses used to develop outlook and situation material prepared within the Department. The Board's objective is to improve the consistency, objectivity, and reliability of the material provided to the public. The Board serves as a focal point for the Departments economic intelligence effort of gathering, interpreting, and summarizing developments affecting domestic and world agriculture. The Board brings together interagency experts to develop official estimates of supply, utilization, and prices for commodities. The Board provides direction in methods used for making estimates and forecasts of domestic and world agriculture, while overseeing remote sensing activity particularly as it relates to food and fiber estimates. The Board participates in planning and developing research programs related to improving departmental forecasting and objective analyses, and coordinates the Department's weather, climate, and related crop monitoring activities.

NATIONAL ENDOWMENT FOR THE ARTS
PERSONNEL DIVISION, ROOM 208
1100 PENNSYLVANIA AVE, NW
WASHINGTON, DC 20506

The goal of the National Endowment for the Arts is the fostering of professional excellence of the arts in America, to nurture and sustain them, and to help create a climate in which they may flourish so they may be experienced and enjoyed by the widest possible public. The Endowment awards grants to individuals, State and regional arts agencies, and nonprofit organizations representing the highest quality in the fields of design arts, dance, expansion arts, folk arts, literature, media arts (film, radio, and television), museums, music, opera, musical theater, theater, and the visual arts. The programs of the National Endowment for the Arts have five basic goals: to foster individual creativity and excellence; to foster institutional creativity and excellence; to preserve the artistic birthright of present and future generations of Americans by supporting survival of the best of all art forms that reflect the American heritage in this full range of cultural and ethnic diversity; to ensure that all Americans have a true opportunity to make an informed, educated choice to have the arts of high quality touch their lives.

NATIONAL ENDOWMENT FOR THE HUMANITIES
DIRECTOR OF PERSONNEL
1100 PENNSYLVANIA AVE, NW
WASHINGTON, DC   20506

The National Endowment for the Humanities is an independent grant-making agency established to support research, education, and public programs in the humanities. According to the agency's authorizing legislation, the term "humanities" includes, but is not limited to, the study of the following: language, both modern and classical; linguistics; literature; history; jurisprudence; philosophy;archeology; comparative religion; ethics; the history, criticism, and theory of the arts; and those aspects of the social sciences that employ historical or philosophical approaches. The Endowment makes grants to individuals, groups, or institutions, schools, colleges, universities, museums, public television stations, libraries, public agencies, and nonprofit private groups- to increase understanding and appreciation of the humanities. Its grant-making is conducted through five operating divisions - Education Programs,

Fellowships and Seminars, General Programs, Research Programs, and State Programs, and two offices, Challenge Grants and Preservation.

AGENCY FOR INTERNATIONAL DEVELOPMENT
CIVIL SERVICE PERSONNEL DIVISION
ROOM 1127, SA-1, 2401 E ST, NW
WASHINGTON, DC 20523

The Agency for International Development (AID) carries out economic assistance programs designed to help the people of developing countries develop their human and economic resources, increase their productive capacities, and improve the quality of human life as well as promote economic and political stability in friendly countries. AID functions under an Administrator, who also currently serves as the Acting Director of the International Development Cooperation Agency. The Administrator directs U.S. foreign and economic assistance operations in more than 60 countries.

OVERSEAS PRIVATE INVESTMENT CORPORATION
FOREIGN SERVICE PERSONNEL DIVISION
OFFICE OF PERSONNEL MANAGEMENT
WASHINGTON, DC 20523

The Overseas Private Investment Corporation (0PIC) assists United States investors to make profitable investments in over 100 developing countries. It encourages investment projects that will help the social and economic development of these countries. At the same time, it helps the U.S. balance of payments through the profits returned to this country, as well as the U.S. jobs and exports created. OPIC offers U.S. investors assistance in finding investment opportunities, insurance to protect their investments, and loans and loan guaranties to help finance their projects.

TRADE AND DEVELOPMENT PROGRAM
OFFICE OF PERSONNEL MANAGEMENT
WASHINGTON, DC 20523

The Trade and Development Program was established to promote economic development in and, simultaneously, export U.S. goods and services to Third World and middle-income developing countries. TDP finances feasibility studies for high priority development projects that will be financed by the World Bank of other international financial institutions or form the host country's own resources. TDP-financed studies are performed only by U.S. firms.

U.S. ARMY CORPS OF ENGINEERS
CIV PERS DIV, ATTEN: CEPE-CS
RM 5105, 20 MASSACHUSETTS AVE, NW
WASHINGTON, DC 20314

The Commanding General, United States Army Corps of Engineers, serves as the Army's Real Property Manager, performing the full cycle of real property activities (requirements, programming, acquisition, operation, maintenance, and disposal); manages and executes engineering, construction, and real estate programs for the Army and the United State Air Force; and performs research and development in support of these programs. He manages and executes Civil Works Programs. These programs include research and development, planning, design, construction, operation and maintenance, and real estate activities related to rivers, harbors, and waterways; administration of laws for protection and preservation of navigable waters and related resources such as wetlands. He also assists in recovery from natural disasters.

U.S. ARMY INFORMATION SYSTEMS COMMAND
CIVILIAN PERSONNEL OFFICE
ARMY GARRISON-FH
FORT HUACHUCA, AZ 85613

The United States Army Information Systems Command is responsible for providing Army Information systems and services worldwide.

MERIT SYSTEMS PROTECTION BOARD
PERSONNEL DIVISION, ROOM 850
1120 VERMONT AVENUE, NW
WASHINGTON, DC   20419

The Merit Systems Protection Board protects the integrity and Federal merit systems and the rights of Federal employees working in the systems. In overseeing the personnel practices of the Federal Government, the Board conducts special studies of the merit system, hears and decides charges of wrongdoing and employee appeals of adverse agency actions, and orders corrective and disciplinary actions against an executive agency or employee when appropriate.

OFFICE OF MANAGEMENT AND BUDGET
DIRECTOR OF PERSONNEL
725 17th STREET NW
WASHINGTON, DC   20503

The Office of Management and Budget (OMB) functions include the following: to assist the President in his program to develop and maintain effective government by reviewing the organizational structure and management procedures of the executive branch to ensure that they produce the intended results; to assist in developing efficient coordinating mechanisms to implement Government activities and to expand interagency cooperation; to assist the President in the preparation of the budget and the formulation of the fiscal program of the Government; to assist the President by clearing and coordinating departmental advice on proposed legislation and by making recommendations as to Presidential action on legislative enactments, in accordance with past practice; to assist in the development of regulatory reform proposals and in programs for paperwork reduction, especially reporting burdens of the public; to assist in the consideration and clearance and, where necessary, in the preparation of proposed Executive orders.

COMMISSION ON CIVIL RIGHTS
PERSONNEL OFFICER
1121 VERMONT AVENUE, NW
WASHINGTON, DC 20425

The United States Commission on Civil Rights is an independent, bipartisan agency first created by the Civil Rights Act of 1957 and reestablished by the United States Commission on Civil Rights Act of 1983. The Commission: investigates allegations in writing under oath or affirmation that certain citizens of the United States are being deprived of their right to vote and have that vote counted by reason of their color, race, religion, sex, age, handicap, or national origin; studies and collects information concerning legal developments constituting discrimination or a denial of equal protection of the laws under the Constitution because of race, color, religion, sex, age, handicap, or national origin or in the administration of justice; appraises the laws and policies of the Federal Government with respect to discrimination or denials of equal protection of the laws under the Constitution because of race, color, religion, sex, age, handicap, or national origin or in the administration of justice.

OFFICE OF THE SECRETARY
OFFICE OF PERSONNEL OPERATIONS
14TH & CONSTITUTION AVE., NW, H1069
WASHINGTON, DC 20230

The Secretary and Deputy Secretary manage and direct policy for the Department of Commerce and provide essential services to keep it operating smoothly.

ECONOMIC DEVELOPMENT ADMINISTRATION
OFFICE OF PERSONNEL OPERATIONS
14TH & CONSTITUTION AVE., NW H1069
WASHINGTON, DC   20230

The Economic Development Administration (EDA) provides loans, grants, and technical assistance to help eligible communities, states, and regions plan and carry out economic development programs. EDA operates primarily where unemployment is high and persistent or where family income is low.

BUREAU OF ECONOMIC ANALYSIS
OFFICE OF PERSONNEL OPERATIONS
14TH & CONSTITUTION AVE, NW, H1069
WASHINGTON, DC   20230

The Bureau of Economic Analysis (BEA) is a source of economic intelligence. BEA provides a clear picture of the economy through the development, preparation and interpretation of the economic accounts of the United States. The economic accounts--national, regional and international--provide basic information on such key issues as economic growth, inflation, regional development and the nation's role in the world economy. National economic accounts include the national income and product accounts of which the gross national product (GNP) is the cornerstone. The national income and product accounts provide a quantitative view of the production, distribution and use of the nation's output. Other branches of the national accounts show the holdings of the nation's tangible wealth and, in input-output accounts, how industries interact to produce the GNP. Regional economic accounts provide information on economic activity by region, state, metropolitan statistical area and county. Estimates of personal income are provided,with detail, by type of income and industry of origin.

INTERNATIONAL TRADE ADMINISTRATION
PERSONNEL OFFICER
14TH AND CONSTITUTION AVE, NW, H4211
WASHINGTON, DC 20230

The International Trade Administration (ITA) carries out the U.S. Government's non-agricultural foreign trade activities. It encourages and promotes U.S. exports of manufactured goods, administers U.S. statutes and agreements dealing with foreign trade and advises on U.S. international trade and commercial policy. ITA's major program areas are: TRADE DEVELOPMENT which is responsible for industry analysis, trade and investment monitoring and statistics, and policy and program development related to specific sectors and industries; INTERNATIONAL ECONOMIC POLICY which is responsible for multilateral and bilateral initiatives and negotiations, as well as for the provision of information and assistance to U.S. businesses investigating or pursuing commercial opportunities in specific foreign countries; and UNITED STATES AND FOREIGN COMMERCIAL SERVICE (US&FCS) which is a worldwide network of 1,300 men and women dedicated to increasing the exports and profits of U.S. companies.The US&FCS is uniquely positioned to help U.S. businesses begin exporting, with direct access to more than 94 percent of the global market for U.S. products.

PATENT AND TRADEMARK OFFICE
OFFICE OF PERSONNEL   CPK-1, SUITE 700
WASHINGTON, DC   20231

The Patent and Trademark Office (PTO) has stimulated national growth by encouraging the invention and disclosure of new technology. In return for the right to exclude others from making, using or selling the invention for 17 years, the inventor discloses to the public detailed information about the invention. The patent examining staff of the Patent and Trademark Office, which consists of approximately 1,400 highly trained engineers and scientists, reviews applications for patents and makes legal determinations concerning the granting of patents. A trademark identifies the producers of goods and services. Trademarks may be renewed indefinitely for periods of 20 years as long as they continue to be used in commerce. Manufacturers seek to achieve a position where the public will associate their trademarks with desirable, high quality merchandise. The trademark examining staff, which consists of over 100 attorneys, examines and applies a variety of legal principles, regulations and court decisions in determining the eligibility of trademarks for registration.

NATIONAL INSTITUTE OF STANDARDS & TECHNOLOGY
PERSONNEL OFFICER
ROOM A-123, ADMINISTRATION BUILDING
GAITHERSBURG, MD   20899

Providing accurate measurements is the unique mission of the National Institute of Standards and Technology, formerly called the National Bureau of Standards. By supplying the measurement foundation for industry, science and technology, the Institute helps the nation improve product quality, achieve higher productivity and increase competitiveness abroad. The science of measurement affects nearly every segment of the U.S. economy--from new technologies such as advanced ceramics, automated manufacturing, superconductivity, electronics and biotechnology to more traditional fields such as weights and measures. For these and other areas of technology, the Institute develops the standards, measurement techniques, reference data, test methods and calibration services that help to ensure national and international measurement capability and compatibility.

U.S. TRAVEL AND TOURISM ADMINISTRATION
OFFICE OF PERSONNEL OPERATIONS
14TH & CONSTITUTION AVE., NW, H1069
WASHINGTON, DC   20230

The United States Travel and Tourism Administration (USTTA) is a small agency with a major mission--to encourage travelers from other countries to visit the United States. Incoming travelers provide profits for U.S.business--increasing the U.S. gross national product and improving the country's balance of payments. USTTA also compiles and publishes statistics on tourist arrivals and departures that provide essential research and marketing tools to governments and the U.S. travel industry.

MINORITY BUSINESS DEVELOPMENT
OFFICE OF PERSONNEL OPERATIONS
14TH & CONSTITUTION AVE, NW, H1069
WASHINGTON, DC 20230

The Minority Business Development Agency (MBDA) promotes minority business as a valuable and dynamic segment of the American free enterprise system, and works to increase minority business ownership, growth and profits. MBDA's broad range of management and technical assistance strengthens the capabilities of minority businesses and promotes partnerships and minority firms with other American businesses, industry and government.

NATIONAL TELECOMMUNICATIONS & INFORMATION
OFFICE OF PERSONNEL OPERATIONS
14TH & CONSTITUTION AVE., NW, H1069
WASHINGTON, DC 20230

The National Telecommunications and Information Administration (NTIA) was established in 1978, incorporating the policymaking functions of the former White House Office of Telecommunications Policy with existing Department telecommunications responsibilities. NTIA continues to be the Executive Branch agency that acts as the President's principal advisor on communications and information policy issues. It is headed by the Assistant Secretary for Communications and Information who also holds the position of NTIA Administrator. NTIA promotes more efficient development of the telecommunications and broadcasting industries; offers technical assistance to minorities in telecommunications; and works to minimize unnecessary U.S. and foreign government interference in international telecommunications markets. NTIA's internationally recognized telecommunications laboratory studies telephone systems and effective radio signal transmissions.

NATIONAL TECHNICAL INFORMATION SERVICE
OFFICE OF PERSONNEL OPERATIONS
5285 PORT ROYAL ROAD
SPRINGFIELD, VA 22161

The National Technical Information Service (NTIS) is a key participant in the development of advanced information products and services for the achievement of U.S. productivity and industrial innovation goals. NTIS is the central source for public sale of U.S. Government-sponsored scientific and technical information. NTIS is a unique government agency supported solely by funds earned from sales. NTIS markets its almost 2 million reports, data files, bibliographic tools and software products to universities, libraries, corporations, research institutions and individuals throughout the world. It manages the Center for the Utilization of Federal Technology and the Federal Software Exchange Center. NTIS is one of the world's leading processors of specialty information.

THE CENSUS
PERSONNEL DIVISION
ROOM 3254, BUILDING THREE
WASHINGTON, DC 20233

The Census Bureau is the nation's foremost statistical agency, gathering information on nearly all facets of American life. Members of the Bureau's staff are involved in planning, conducting, analyzing, evaluating and publishing censuses on agriculture, business, construction and housing, foreign trade, manufacturing, transportation and government. The Bureau is also widely recognized for its research in statistical sampling and methodologies. The Decennial Census of population is used to determine the delineation of Congressional districts and to determine the number of Congressional representatives. The population census also determines the amount of Federal funds received by various enumeration districts.

ECONOMIC AFFAIRS UNITS
OFFICE OF PERSONNEL OPERATIONS
14TH & CONSTITUTION AVE., NW, H1069
WASHINGTON, DC 20230

The Under Secretary for Economic Affairs leads Commerce's participation in developing Executive Branch economic policy. Major activities include interpreting economic conditions and trends, analyzing business and economic implications of developments and proposed policies, providing basic economic and demographic statistics and encouraging economic growth through technological innovation.

COMMODITY FUTURES TRADING COMMISSION
DIRECTOR OF PERSONNEL
2033 K STREET, ROOM 202
WASHINGTON, DC 20581

The Commodity Futures Trading Commission consists of five major operating components: the divisions of enforcement, economic analysis, trading and markets, and the offices of the executive director and the general counsel. The Commission regulates trading on the 11 U.S. futures exchanges, which offer active futures and options contracts. It also regulates the activities of numerous commodity exchange members, public brokerage houses (futures commission merchants), Commission-registered futures industry salespeople and associated persons, commodity trading advisors, and commodity pool operators. The Commission's regulatory and enforcement efforts are designed to ensure that the futures trading process is fair and that it protects both the rights of customers and the financial integrity of the marketplace. CFTC approves the rules under which an exchange proposes to operate and monitors exchange enforcement of those rules. It reviews the terms of proposed futures contracts, and registers companies and individuals who handle customer funds or give trading advice.

FEDERAL BUREAU OF INVESTIGATION
APPLICANT COORDINATOR
10th AND PENNSYLVANIA AVENUE, NW
WASHINGTON, DC 20520

Federal Bureau of Investigation (FBI) serves as the investigative arm of the Department of Justice. The FBI has jurisdiction over 200 types of cases, including white-collar crime, organized crime, foreign counterintelligence, public corruption, civil rights violations, terrorism, Federal drug violations, kidnapping, bank robbery and interstate criminal activity. The FBI also works with other Federal, state and local law enforcement agencies to investigate matters of joint interest. Through its forensic laboratories, fingerprint files and National Crime Information Center, the FBI acts as a resource and clearinghouse for local and state law enforcement agencies throughout the United States. Federal Bureau of Investigation positions are not part of the regular Civil Service competitive system, and the Office of Personnel Management does not accept applications for these positions. All employees must be available for assignments which may require overtime, night or weekend duty. Prospective FBI employees are required to submit to urinalysis for drug abuse prior to employment.

IMMIGRATION AND NATURALIZATION SERVICE
PERSONNEL DIVISION
425 I STREET, NW, ROOM 6023
WASHINGTON, DC 20536

Under the Immigration and Nationality Act, the Immigration and Naturalization Service is both a law enforcement and service-oriented agency with responsibilities ranging from admitting, excluding, investigating, and deporting aliens to guiding and assisting them in gaining entry to the United States, receiving benefits, and becoming naturalized citizens. In addition, the 1986 amendment to the Act calls for the Service to administer programs whereby up to 2 million illegal aliens may become lawful residents. Specifically, the Service inspects aliens to determine their admissibility for entry to the United States; accords preference visa classifications to relatives of U.S. citizens and residents, as well as to needed workers; changes the status of aliens from non-immigrant to permanent resident; processes refugees overseas for resettlement in the United States; examines applicants for U.S. citizenship; prevents illegal entry; investigates, apprehends, detains and deports aliens who violate immigration laws; and works with other Federal, state and local law enforcement agencies to stem the flow of illegal drugs to the country.

DRUG ENFORCEMENT ADMINISTRATION
OFFICE OF PERSONNEL
700 ARMY NAVY DRIVE, ROOM W-3162
ARLINGTON, VA   22202

The Drug Enforcement Administration (DEA) is the lead Federal law enforcement agency having the responsibility of combating drug abuse. DEA was established to control narcotics and dangerous-drug abuse more effectively through enforcement and prevention. In carrying out its mission, DEA cooperates with other Federal agencies, with foreign as well as state and local governments, private industry and other organizations. Its objectives are to reach all levels of the source of supply and to seize the greatest possible quantity of illegal drugs before they reach the user. To achieve its mission, DEA has stationed highly trained agents along the numerous routes of illicit traffic, both in the United States and in foreign countries. DEA Special Agents conduct criminal investigations and prepare for the prosecution of major violators of the drug laws of the United States. Entry-level salary is at the GS-7 or GS-9 level, depending on the applicant's qualifications, with additional overtime compensation. Careers generally progress to the GS-12 level in three years.

EXPORT-IMPORT BANK OF U.S.
PERSONNEL,
811 VERMONT AVE, NW
WASHINGTON, DC   20571

The Export-Import Bank is the independent U.S. Government agency that facilitates the export financing of U.S. goods and services. It supplements and encourages but does not compete with commercial financing. By neutralizing the effect of export credit subsidies from other governments and by absorbing risks that the private sector will not accept, Eximbank enables U.S. exporters to compete fairly in overseas markets on the basis of price, performance, delivery, and services. To achieve its export finance mission, Eximbank has authority to provide loans, guarantees and insurance. The bank's policies are coordinated with overall U.S. government foreign and economic policy objectives. To be eligible for Eximbank's support, goods or services exported must be at least 50 percent U.S. content. Eximbank has helped new exporters to break into foreign markets for the first time and has helped established exporters to sustain their overseas markets in the midst of international financial uncertainties and intense foreign competition.

EQUAL EMPLOYMENT OPPORTUNITY COMMISSION
JOB INFORMATION CENTER
PERSONNEL MANAGEMENT SERVICES
1801 L STREET, NW
WASHINGTON, DC 20507

The US Equal Employment Opportunity Commission was created by Title VII of the Civil Rights Act of 1964, which prohibits employment discrimination based on race, color, religion, sex or national origin. In 20 years, EEOC has seen the number of employment-related discrimination complaints rise from 8,800 to nearly 70,000 annually. As the primary enforcement agency for equal employment opportunity laws, EEOC has adopted significant policies to ensure certainty and predictability of enforcement, to attain the fullest relief possible for victims of discrimination and to ensure timely and complete compliance with investigations by uncooperative respondents. The Commission has five members and a General Counsel who are appointed by the President and confirmed by the U.S. Senate. The Chairman, designated by the President, is responsible for the administrative operations of the agency, including the implementation of policy and procedures established by the Commission to carry out the laws it enforces.

FEDERAL EMERGENCY MANAGEMENT AGENCY HEADQUARTERS
OPERATIONS DIVISION OFFICE OF PERSONNEL
ROOM 816   500 C STREET, SW
WASHINGTON, DC 20472

The Federal Emergency Management Agency was created to provide a single point of accountability for all Federal emergency preparedness, mitigation, and response activities.The Agency is chartered to enhance the multiple use of emergency preparedness and response resources at the Federal, State, and local levels of government in preparing for and responding to the full range of emergencies-natural, technological, and attack-related-and to integrate into a comprehensive framework activities concerned with hazard mitigation, preparedness planning, relief operations, and recovery assistance.

ENVIRONMENTAL PROTECTION AGENCY
RECRUITMENT CENTER (PM-224)
401 M STREET. SW
WASHINGTON, DC 20460

The mission of the United States Environmental Protection Agency (EPA) is to protect the health and welfare of the American people by preventing, abating and cleaning up pollution hazards. The Agency endeavors to accomplish its mission systematically by proper integration of a variety of research, monitoring, standard-setting and enforcement activities. Overall, EPA strives to formulate and implement policies which lead to a compatible balance between human activities and the ability of natural systems to support and nurture life. EPA was created in 1970 through an executive reorganization plan devised to consolidate the Federal government's environmental regulatory activities into a single agency. EPA is headed by an Administrator who is supported by a Deputy Administrator, two Associate Administrators, nine Assistant Administrators, a General Counsel, and the Inspector General.

FEDERAL DEPOSIT INSURANCE CORPORATION
DIRECTOR OF PERSONNEL
550 17th STREET, NW
WASHINGTON, DC 20429

The Federal Deposit Insurance Corporation (FDIC) has served as an integral part of the nation's financial system for more than 50 years. While the agency has grown and modified its operations in response to changing economic conditions and shifts in the banking environment, the mission of the FDIC over the past five decades has remained unchanged: to insure bank deposits and to reduce the economic disruptions caused by bank failures. Unlike most Federal agencies, FDIC does not receive funds from the U.S. Congress. The Corporation's income is generated primarily by regular assessments that banks pay for insurance and by FDIC's earnings from investments. On the average, 40 percent of the Corporation's staff is comprised of Bank Examiners organizationally assigned to the Division of Bank Supervision. Working in teams, these Examiners seek to determine the financial condition of a bank, the adequacy of its internal procedures and the character of its management. Once their review is completed, Examiners discuss findings with bank management and make appropriate recommendations.

FARM CREDIT ADMINISTRATION
HUMAN RESOURCES DIVISION
1501 FARM CREDIT DRIVE
MCLEAN, VA 22102

The Farm Credit Administration is responsible for the regulation and examination of borrower-owned banks and associations and their service organizations that comprise the cooperative Farm Credit System. These institutions are the Federal land banks, which make long-term loans on farm or rural real estate, or real estate connected with a commercial fisherman's operation, through local Federal land bank associations; the Federal intermediate credit banks providing short and intermediate-term loan funds to production credit associations and other institutions financing farmers, ranchers, rural homeowners, owners of farm related businesses, and commercial fisherman; and the banks for cooperatives that make loans of all kinds to agricultural and aquatic cooperatives. The loan funds provided borrowers by these institutions are obtained primarily through the sale of securities to investors in the Nation's capital markets. As the preferred processes for settling issues between employers and representatives of employees; developing the art, science, and practice of dispute resolution; and fostering constructive joint relationships of labor and management leaders to increase their mutual understanding and solution of common problems.

ALCOHOL, DRUG ABUSE & MENTAL HEALTH
PERSONNEL OFFICE
5600 FISHERS LANE, ROOM 12-95
ROCKVILLE, MD   20859

The Alcohol, Drug Abuse and Mental Health Administration (ADAMHA) is the lead Federal agency in the national effort to prevent, control, and treat alcohol and drug problems, and mental and emotional illnesses. The agency conducts clinical and biochemical research in its own laboratories, and supports research by scientists working in a variety of disciplines in universities, medical schools, hospitals and drug abuse and mental health treatment centers. In addition, ADAMHA provides support, through a Block Grant that provides Federal funds to be managed by the states, to help states establish and operate alcohol, drug abuse and mental health programs. ADAMHA disseminates information to health professionals and the public. To carry out its responsibilities, ADAMHA employs approximately 2,000 individuals such as Physicians, Psychologists, Sociologists, Social Workers, Research Scientists, Community Workers and Educators.

HEALTH RESOURCES AND SERVICES ADMINISTRATION
OFFICE OF PERSONNEL
5600 FISHERS LANE, ROOM 14A-46
ROCKVILLE, MD 20857

The Health Resources and Services Administration (HRSA)provides leadership and direction to programs and activities designed to improve the health services for people of the United States and to develop health care and maintenance systems which are adequately financed, comprehensive, interrelated and responsive to the needs of individuals and families at all levels of society. HRSA is comprised of the following Bureaus: Bureau of Health Care Delivery and Assistance, Bureau of Health Professions, Bureau of Maternal and Child Health and Bureau of Resources Development. Approximately 2,700 individuals are employed by HRSA. The

The occupations utilized are accounting, budget analysis, administration, and public health program administration. The HRSA locations include its Headquarters in Rockville, Maryland, and 10 Regional Offices.

TOXIC SUBSTANCES AND DISEASES
PERSONNEL OFFICE
1600 CLIFTON ROAD, NE
ATLANTA, GA 30333

The mission of ATSDR is to carry out the health-related responsibilities of the Comprehensive Environmental Response, Compensation, and Liability Act of 1980 and the Resource Conservation and Recovery Act provisions of the Solid Waste Disposal Act. To accomplish its mission, ATSDR determines the extent of danger to the public health from a release or threat of release of a hazardous substance by conducting a health assessment of the situation, establishing and maintaining disease and exposure registries and establishing and maintaining an inventory of information on the health effects of toxic substances. In addition, it maintains a listing of areas closed or otherwise restricted to the public because of contamination from toxic substances and provides consultation and coordination with private or public health care providers in medical care and testing. ATSDR works closely with the Environmental Protection Agency (EPA) in identifying hazardous waste substances to be regulated and in issuing EPA periodic reports.

FOOD AND DRUG ADMINISTRATION
DIVISION OF PERSONNEL MANAGEMENT
5600 FISHERS LANE, ROOM 4B-41
ROCKVILLE, MD 20857

The Food and Drug Administration (FDA) is the regulatory agency concerned with protecting the health and well-being of the American consumer by monitoring and regulating consumer products. It monitors the food, drug and cosmetic industries; studies labeling and packaging practices; and checks radiation levels of consumer products and equipment to ensure their safety for human use. FDA is comprised of six Centers: Center for Food Safety and Applied Nutrition, Center for Drug Evaluation and Research, Center for Biologics Evaluation and Research, Center for Veterinary Medicine, Center for Devices and Radiological Health and National Center for Toxicological Research.

INDIAN HEALTH SERVICE
PERSONNEL OPERATIONS BRANCH
5600 FISHERS LANE, ROOM 6A-15
ROCKVILLE, MD   20857

The Indian Health Service (IHS) provides comprehensive health services for more than 900,000 Indians and Alaska Natives. The IHS program is community oriented and comprehensive, offering preventive, curative and rehabilitative services. Included, in addition to general medical and dental care, are such services as maternal and child health, eye care, diabetes, family planning, mental health, social services, alcoholism, nutrition, public health nursing, health education and environmental health and sanitation. The goal of the Indian Health Service is to raise the health status of the American Indians and Alaska Natives to the highest possible level.

CENTERS FOR DISEASE CONTROL
PERSONNEL OFFICE
1600 CLIFTON ROAD, NE
ATLANTA, GA   30333

The Centers for Disease Control (CDC) provides leadership and direction for a broad range of programs designed to safeguard and improve the health of the American people.   CDC works to prevent and control infectious and chronic diseases; to prevent disease, disability and death associated with environmental and workplace hazards; and to promote health and reduce health risks through education and information. The agency also supports local, state, national and international disease prevention efforts in epidemiology, disease surveillance, laboratory science and training. ODC has six major operational units: National Institute for Occupational Safety and Health, Center for Health, Promotion and Education, Center for Prevention Services, Center for Environmental Health, Center for Infectious Diseases and National Center for Health Statistics.

OFFICE OF INSPECTOR GENERAL
PERSONNEL OPERATIONS GROUP B
330 INDEPENDENCE AVENUE, SW
WASHINGTON, DC 20201

Pursuant to the Inspector General Act of 1978, the Inspector General is appointed by the President with the advice and consent of the Senate to keep the Secretary and the Congress informed of fraud and other deficiencies in the Department's programs and operations. The Office of Inspector General is responsible for conducting independent audits and investigations relating to the Department's operations. The

Inspector General also provides leadership and coordination for activities designed to promote economy, efficiency, and effectiveness in the administration of programs and operations, as well as the prevention and detection of fraud and abuse in such programs and operations.

U.S. INFORMATION AGENCY
OFFICE OF PERSONNEL
301 FOURTH STREET, SW
WASHINGTON, DC 20547

The U.S. Information Agency (USIA) was established in 1953 as an administratively autonomous agency within the Executive Branch and is responsible for the Government's overseas information, educational exchange and cultural programs. USIA's Director reports to the President and receives policy guidance from the Secretary of State. Overseas, USIA is known as the U.S. Information Service (USIS). The Agency administers a wide variety of information, educational and cultural programs around the world with the main purpose of strengthening communication between Americans and the people of other nations. USIA's work is carried out by its nearly 900 Foreign Service Officers assigned to 205 posts in 127 countries overseas, with support provided by 3,973 employees in Washington, DC.

OFFICE OF THE SECRETARY
PERSONNEL OFFICE (PPS-P), MS-5459
WASHINGTON, DC 22040

The Secretary directs and supervises operations and activities of the Department. The Secretary also has certain supervisory responsibilities relating to territorial governments. The Office of the Secretary includes various offices that provide advice and assistance to the Secretariat, which is comprised of the Under Secretary, the Solicitor and Assistant Secretaries. The Office also includes "Other Departmental Offices," referring to a number of units that carry out special programs.

BUREAU OF LAND MANAGEMENT
DIVISION OF PERSONNEL, MS-3619
18th AND C STREETS, NW (MIB)
WASHINGTON, DC 20240

The Bureau of Land Management (BLM) is responsible for the management, conservation and development of the resources on more than 270 million acres of public land. The BLM also administers mining and mineral leasing on an additional 300 million acres of Federal, state, and private land. FLPMA established that public lands are to be managed under principles of multiple use and sustained yield. Renewable and non-renewable resources of the public lands include range, timber, minerals, watershed, recreation, wildlife, aquatic habitat, archeological deposits and wilderness. In order to manage, conserve and develop the public domain for the multiple use of these resources, BLM has a wide range of resource management activities that require the skills and services of many professions and occupations. BLM is responsible for administering rangeland; carrying out resource management programs; providing recreation areas; issuing leases and overseeing operations for oil, gas and other mineral development on public land; selling timber from BLM administered lands; maintaining public land records and performing cadastral survey and resurvey.

BUREAU OF INDIAN AFFAIRS
PERSONNEL MGMT., HQ., MS-320SIB
1951 CONSTITUTION AVENUE, NW
WASHINGTON, DC 20240

The Bureau of Indian Affairs (BIA) is the Federal agency with primary responsibility for working with Indian tribal governments and Alaska Native village communities. Other Federal agencies may deal with Indians or Alaska Natives as members of an ethnic group or simply as individuals, but the BIA is distinctive in that it deals with them as governments in a government-to-government relationship. The key objectives of the Bureau are to encourage Indian and Alaska Native people to manage their own affairs under a trust relationship with the Federal Government and to facilitate the development of their human and natural resource potential. The Bureau provides a variety of programs to the Indian people and funding to an increasing number of tribes that wish to manage these programs themselves on a contractual basis. The Bureau's trust responsibilities include: the protection of Indian rights in their trust property and those rights affecting trust property that are afforded by tribal sovereignty.

OFFICE OF SURFACE MINING
DIVISION OF PERSONNEL, ROOM 44-S
1951 CONSTITUTION AVENUE, NW
WASHINGTON, DC 20240

The Office of Surface Mining Reclamation and Enforcement (OSM) was established in the Department of the Interior by the Surface Mining Control and Reclamation Act of 1977. The OSM's main objectives, now that most coal mining states have assumed prime responsibility for regulating coal mining reclamation activities within their borders, are to oversee mining and reclamation in these states, to assist the states in meeting the objectives of the Act, and to regulate mining and reclamation activities in the states that choose not to assume prime responsibility.

MINERAL MANAGEMENT SERVICE
PERSONNEL DIVISION, MS 2400
381 ELDEN STREET
HERNDON, VA 22070

In July 1981, the Commission on Fiscal Accountability of the Nation's Energy Resources was directed to investigate the alleged loss of millions of dollars in royalty revenues from mineral leases because of inadequate accounting controls and field inspection practices. The result of the Commission's investigation was a report consisting of 60 recommendations submitted to the Secretary in January 1982. As recommended by the Commission, on January 19, 1982, the Minerals Management Service (MMS) was established from existing organizations as a separate Bureau within the Department of the Interior. The MMS handles leasing and resource management functions for the nation's Outer Continental Shelf, and for submerged lands off the coasts with the potential to supply a significant portion of this nation's future oil and gas needs. The Service leases offshore areas for exploration and production and closely monitors drilling and production to protect the coastal environments and ensure proper royalty collection.

ACTION
PERSONNEL MGT DIV - 5TH FLOOR
1100 VERMONT AVE, NW
WASHINGTON, DC 20525

ACTION is the Federal domestic volunteer agency whose mission is to stimulate and to expand voluntary citizen participation. The Agency, through support of its established programs and of local volunteer efforts, challenges Americans to use their energies and skills to address the needs of communities around the country, particularly needs related to the poor, the disadvantaged and the elderly. ACTION was established in July 1971, and provides volunteer opportunities for Americans from all walks of life. The diversity of ACTION programs allows for part-time or full-time service up to two years, with some volunteers serving on stipends and others on a non-paid basis.

NATIONAL SCIENCE FOUNDATION
DIVISION OF PERSONNEL
1800 G STREET, NW, ROOM 208
WASHINGTON, DC 20550

The National Science Foundation's (NSF) aim is to promote and advance scientific progress in the United States. It is responsible for the overall health of science across all disciplines. NSF receives more than 30,000 proposals each year for research, graduate fellowships and math/science/engineering education; it makes more than 13,000 awards. These go to universities, colleges, academic consortia, non-profit institutions and small businesses. The Foundation also aids cooperative research between universities and industry and U.S. participation in international scientific efforts. NSF is structured much as is a university, with grant-making divisions for the various disciplines and fields of science and engineering. The Foundation's staff is helped by advisors, primarily from the scientific community, who serve on formal committees or as ad hoc reviewers of proposals. This advisory system, which focuses on both program direction and specific proposals, involves more than 50,000 scientists and engineers a year.

NATIONAL LABOR RELATIONS BOARD
PERSONNEL OPERATIONS
1717 PENNSYLVANIA AVENUE, NW
WASHINGTON, DC 20570

The mission of the National Labor Relations Board (NLRB), an independent agency of the Federal Government, is to protect the public interest by minimizing industrial strife. It accomplishes its objectives by encouraging collective bargaining between representatives of employees and employers and by protecting the rights of employees to organize into groups of their own choosing. The NLRB has two main functions: to prevent and remedy unfair labor practices, whether committed by labor organizations or employers; and to establish, usually by secret-ballot elections, whether certain groups of employees wish to be represented by labor organizations for collective-bargaining purposes.

NATIONAL ARCHIVES AND RECORDS ADMINISTRATION
PERSONNEL OPERATIONS BRANCH
9700 PAGE BOULEVARD
ST. LOUIS, MO 63132

The National Archives and Records Administration is responsible for establishing policies and procedures for managing the records of the United States Government. The National Archives assists Federal agencies in adequately documenting their activities, administering their records management programs, scheduling their records, and retiring their noncurrent records to Federal Records Centers. The agency also accessions, arranges, describes, preserves, and makes available to the public the historically valuable records of all three branches of the Government. Managing the Presidential Libraries system, assisting the National Historical Publications and Records Commission in its grant program for State and local records and edited publications of prominent Americans, and publishing the laws, regulations, Presidential, and other public documents are also key functions of the National Archives and Records Administration.

NATIONAL SECURITY COUNCIL
RECRUITMENT BRANCH
ATTN: M322
FORT MEADE, MD 20755

The National Security Council was established by the National Security Act of 1947, as amended by the National Security Act Amendments of 1949. By Reorganization Plan No. 4 of 1949, the Council was placed in the Executive Office of the President. The National Security Council is chaired by the President. Its statutory members, in addition to the President, are the Vice President and the Secretaries of State and Defense. The Chairman of the Joint Chiefs of Staff is the statutory military adviser to the Council, and the Director of Central Intelligence is its intelligence adviser. The statutory function of the Council is to advise the President with respect to the integration of domestic, foreign, and military policies relating to national security.

NUCLEAR REGULATORY COMMISSION
COLLEGE RECRUITMENT COORDINATOR
OFFICE OF PERSONNEL
WASHINGTON, DC 20555

The Nuclear Regulatory Commission (NRC) was established in January 1975, under provisions of the Energy Reorganization Act of 1974, which abolished the Atomic Energy Commission and transferred regulatory responsibilities to the NRC. Since its inception, the agency has grown to a total of 3,400 employees, at Headquarters and in regional offices in King of Prussia, Pennsylvania; Atlanta, Georgia; Glen Ellyn, Illinois; Arlington, Texas; and Walnut Creek, California. The independent regulatory agency has as its primary mission regulating uses of nuclear energy to protect the health and safety of the public and environment. NRC has developed a comprehensive program of regulation, licensing and enforcement. NRC also oversees research programs of Federal and private research organizations. The licensing of nuclear power reactors and the individuals who operate those facilities is one of the principle efforts of the NRC.

U.S. OFFICE OF PERSONNEL MANAGEMENT
1900 E STREET, NW
WASHINGTON, DC 20415

The U.S. Office of Personnel Management (OPM) is the central agency responsible for establishing Federal human resources policy and for providing leadership and policy guidance to the Federal departments and agencies in the area of personnel management. The Office of Personnel Management administers a merit system for Federal employment that includes recruiting, examining, training and promoting people on the basis of their knowledge and skills regardless of their race, religion, sex, political affiliation, physical disability or other non-merit factors. The Office's role also is to ensure that the Federal Government provides an array of personnel services to applicants and employees. Through a wide range of programs designed to develop and to foster employee effectiveness, the Office supports Government program managers in their human resources responsibilities and provides benefits to employees and to retired employees and their survivors. OPM administers one of the world's largest pension systems and is responsible for the management of the nation's largest group health and life insurance programs.

PEACE CORPS
OFFICE OF PERSONNEL
1900 K STREET, NW, ROOM 7007
WASHINGTON, DC 20526

Founded in 1961 by President John F. Kennedy, the Peace Corps is the international development agency of the Federal Government. It places volunteers in countries throughout the developing world in projects including education, health and nutrition, community development, small-business development, agriculture, fisheries and forestry. Volunteers must be at least 18 years old, but there is no upper age limit. The agency has staff in both the United States and in the countries where the volunteers serve. The staff members work in all areas associated with business, including administration, finance, computers and training. The Peace Corps staff trains volunteers in personal relationships, in cultural sensitivity to country-specific customs and in the specific skills required for their assignments. In addition, staff members perform liaison with the countries that host volunteers.

FEDERAL RETIREMENT THRIFT INVESTMENT BOARD
PERSONNEL OFFICER
805 15th STREET, NW
WASHINGTON, DC 20005

The Federal Retirement Thrift Investment Board is responsible for the operation of the Thrift Savings Plan. The Thrift Savings Plan is a tax-deferred defined contribution plan that was established as one of the three parts of the Federal Employees' Retirement System (FERS). For employees covered under FERS, savings accumulated through the Plan make an important addition to the retirement benefits provided by Social Security and the FERS Basic Annuity. Civil Service Retirement System employees can also take advantage of the Plan to supplement their annuities. The Board operates the Thrift Savings Plan and manages the investments of the Thrift Savings Fund solely for the benefit of participants and their beneficiaries. As part of these responsibilities, the Board maintains as account for each Plan participant, makes loans, purchases annuity contracts, and provides for the payment of benefits.

RAILROAD RETIREMENT BOARD
BUREAU OF PERSONNEL
844 RUSH STREET
CHICAGO, IL 60611

This agency was created by legislation in the 1930s to administer the nation's railroad pension plans while the Social Security system was still in the planning stage. The Board currently pays retirement-survivor benefits to almost a million annuitants and unemployment-sickness benefits to more than 100,000 beneficiaries. The primary source of income for the railroad retirement-survivor benefit program is payroll taxes paid by the railroad employers and their employees, while the income for the unemployment-sickness program is provided solely by the railroads. The Board employs Claims Examiners to adjudicate claims for benefits; Field Representatives to assist railroad personnel in filing claims; Auditors and Criminal Investigators to ensure the integrity of the programs, and Computer Specialists to develop and maintain effective systems for processing claims and for the Board's administrative programs. The Board also employs Actuaries, Attorneys, Personnel Specialists and other staff as required by an independent Federal agency in the Executive Branch of the Government. Opportunities for advancement are good.

SMALL BUSINESS ADMINISTRATION
CENTRAL PERSONNEL OFFICE
1441 L STREET, NW, ROOM 300
WASHINGTON, DC 20416

The Small Business Administration (SBA) aids, counsels and assists small businesses in order to preserve and protect free enterprise. Specific activities of the Small Business Administration include: helping individuals obtain loans to restore or to replace businesses and homes damaged or destroyed by storms, floods or other disasters; conferences, workshops and problem solving clinics, held in cooperation with universities, colleges and Chambers of Commerce, for small business owners; helping small firms owned by handicapped, or socially or economically disadvantaged individuals become more competitive through business education; assisting small businesses in preparing bids and obtaining Federal contracts; working with small-business exporters to help them obtain business loans.

SECURITIES AND EXCHANGE COMMISSION
OFFICE OF PERSONNEL
450 FIFTH STREET, NW
WASHINGTON, DC 20549

The SEC is an independent, non-partisan, quasi-judicial regulatory agency. The Commission's principal responsibilities are the administration and enforcement of Federal securities laws. The Commission regulates the nation's securities markets, stock brokers, investment companies and investment advisors, and prescribes certain requirements for companies that issue stock or other securities. The Commission also serves as advisor to Federal Courts in corporate reorganization proceedings under Chapter 11 of the Bankruptcy Reform Act of 1978 and, in cases begun prior to October 1, 1979, Chapter X of the National Bankruptcy Act. The Commission reports annually to Congress on the administration of the securities laws. The Commission carries out its work from both its Washington Headquarters and the Regional Offices charged with specific responsibilities under the securities laws. Additionally, there are offices responsible for the smooth and effective administration of the Commission itself. Overall responsibility for carrying out the SEC's mission rests with the Commissioners.

NATIONAL GALLERY OF ART
OFFICE OF PERSONNEL
6TH AND CONSTITUTION AVE., NW
WASHINGTON DC 20565

The National Gallery of Art is governed by a Board of Trustees composed of five Trustees and the Secretary of State, the Secretary of the Treasury, the Chief Justice of the United States, and the Secretary of the Smithsonian Institution. It houses one of the finest collections in the world, illustrating Western man's achievements in painting, sculpture, and the graphic arts. The collections, beginning with the 13th century, are rich in European old master paintings and French, Spanish, Italian, American, and British 18th-19th century paintings; sculpture from the late Middle Ages to the present; Renaissance medals and bronzes; Chinese porcelains; and over 75,000 works of graphic art from the 12th to the 20th centuries. The collections continue to be built by private donation rather than by the expenditure of government funds, which serve solely to operate and maintain the building and its collections.

WOODROW WILSON INTERNATIONAL CENTER
370 L'ENFANT PROMENADE
PERSONNEL OFFICE - SUITE 704
WASHINGTON DC 20024

The Woodrow Wilson International Center for Scholars seeks, through open, international competition, outstanding project proposals representing diverse scholarly interests and approaches from individuals throughout the world. The Center welcomes all disciplines and scholarship that transcends narrow specialties and includes a strong humanistic component. Fellows engage in no sponsored, classified, or structured group research at the Center.

Administrative Careers *with* America

U.S. Office of Personnel Management

Qualification Information
Statement QI-B
Rev. August 1990
Previous edition usable

Business, Finance and Management Occupations
Grades GS-5 and GS-7

Applications are accepted for these occupations on an as-needed basis. To determine if applications are being accepted, contact the College Hotline (900-990-9200) or the closest OPM office (look in the telephone directory under U.S. Government).

The Federal Government needs persons with potential for advancement into responsible professional and administrative jobs. If you have a college degree or equivalent experience, this examination offers you the opportunity to compete for various positions in the business, finance and program management fields with Federal agencies across the country. Many positions are filled at grade GS-5 and do not require specialized education or experience. If you meet certain academic standards, you may apply directly to agencies to be considered without having to take the written test. For more information on this option refer to the section titled *Application Procedures*.

This examination is one of six which is used to fill entry-level professional and administrative positions. The five other examinations are:
- Health, Safety and Environmental Occupations
- Writing and Public Information Occupations
- Personnel, Administration and Computer Occupations
- Benefits Review, Tax and Legal Occupations
- Law Enforcement and Investigation Occupations

The Office of Personnel Management (OPM) examines for many other occupations at the entry level, and at higher grade levels. To obtain information on these and other Federal jobs see the section titled *Further Information*.

Jobs Filled Through This Examination

Agricultural Programs*: *Includes*
  Agricultural Marketing
  Agricultural Program Specialist
Business: *Includes*
  Appraising and Assessing
  Bond Sales Promotion
  Budget Analysis
  Building Management
  Financial Administration and Programs
  Food Assistance Program Specialist
  General Business and Industry
  Housing Management
  Public Utilities Specialist
  Realty
  Wage and Hour Law Administration
Communication (Telecommunications) Specialist*
Contract Specialist*
Financial Institution Examining*
Finance*: *Includes*
  Financial Analysis
  Insurance Examining
  Loan Specialist
Industrial Programs*: *Includes*
  Industrial Property Management
  Industrial Specialist
  Quality Assurance Specialist

Supply: *Includes*
  Distribution Facilities and Storage Management
  General Supply
  Inventory Management
  Logistics Management
  Packaging
  Property Disposal
  Supply Cataloging
  Supply Program Management
Trade Specialist*
Transportation*: *Includes*
  Highway Safety Management
  Traffic Management
  Transportation Industry Analysis
  Transportation Operations
  Transportation Specialist
Unemployment Insurance*
An asterisk (*) denotes positions with specific qualification requirements.

Best Opportunities—The options offering the best opportunities for employment are: Business, Contract Specialist, Industrial Programs, and Supply.

Qualification Information

The requirements for these positions vary. To qualify for those positions **without** an asterisk (*), you must meet the conditions listed under *Basic Requirements*. To qualify for those positions **with** an asterisk (*), you must meet the conditions for the particular position listed under *Specific Requirements*.

Basic Requirements

1. Grade GS-5 Positions:
   Four years of education leading to a bachelor's degree, 3 years of responsible experience, or an equivalent combination of education and experience.

2. Grade GS-7 Positions:
   a. A bachelor's degree and one of the following Superior Academic Achievement provisions:
     — A grade average of "B" (a GPA of 3.0 or higher) for all completed undergraduate courses, or those completed in the last 2 years of undergraduate study.
     — A grade average of "B+" (a GPA of 3.5 or higher) for all courses in your major field of study, or those courses in your major completed in the last 2 years of undergraduate study.
     — Rank in the upper one-third of your class in the college, university, or major subdivision.
     — Membership in a national honorary scholastic society (other than freshman honor societies) recognized by the Association of College Honor Societies; or
   b. One full year of graduate education, law school, or a graduate degree; or

2

c. One year of work experience in a field related to the position. The experience must be equivalent to the GS-5 level or higher in the Federal service; or

d. An equivalent combination of education and experience.

Specific Requirements

The amount of education and/or experience required is the same as spelled out in the *Basic Requirements*. However, the area of education and experience must meet specific requirements as spelled out for each occupation listed. (Education is defined as a major in the field or 24 semester hours [36 quarter hours] in the field.)

Positions, and their specialized requirements, are listed below.

• Agricultural Marketing

The education must be in one of the following fields: Accounting, Agriculture or related fields, Agriculture Economics, Business Administration, Commerce, Economics, Marketing, Mathematics, Statistics, or Transportation.

The experience must be related to the practices of marketing agricultural products, the preparation of mathematical, statistical, or economic reports, or involve the basic principles of agricultural or physical sciences.

For grade GS-7 positions the experience must be related to agricultural marketing.

• Agricultural Program Specialist

The education must be in one of the following fields: Agriculture or related fields, Agriculture Economics, Agronomy, Business Administration, Economics, or Marketing.

The experience must be related to the production or marketing of agricultural commodities.

• Communications (Telecommunications) Specialist

The education must be in one of the following fields: Business Administration, Computer Science, Electrical or Electronic Engineering, Information Systems, Industrial Management, Mathematics, Physics, Public Utilities, Statistics, or Telecommunications.

The experience must be related to the functions, problems and/or solutions of telecommunications systems.

Alternate Requirements: You may qualify if you have 48 or more months of training above the high school level in communications, electronics, or data processing. The training must include work at an advanced level.

• Contract Specialist

The education may be in any field.

The experience must be related to purchasing, procurement, or business management. Additionally, the following certifications are qualifying: Certified Professional Contracts Manager (from the National Contract Management Association), Certified Purchasing Manager (from the National Association of Purchasing Management), Certified Public Purchasing Officer (from the National Instutute of Governmental Purchasing).

For grade GS-7 positions, the experience must be in or directly related to contracting work.

• Financial Institution Examining

The education must be in one of the following fields: Accounting, Banking, Business Administration, Commercial or Banking Law, Economics, Finance, or other field related to the position.

The experience must be related to accounting or auditing. At the grade GS-7 level, the experience must be related to accounting or auditing of financial institutions, involve professional accounting or auditing work, or provide knowledge of laws applicable to financial institutions.

Alternative requirements: A CPA certificate (Certified Public Accountant) meets all GS-5 requirements.

• Financial Analysis, Insurance Examining, and Loan Specialist

The education must be in one of the following fields: Accounting, Agriculture or related fields, Banking, Business Administration, Finance, Economics, Engineering, Insurance, Law, Mathematics, Real Estate, Statistics, or other related field.

The experience must be related to the financial or insurance fields, or involve gathering and analyzing facts or figures.

For grade GS-7 Financial Analyst, the experience must provide a knowledge of corporate finance, and the financial and management structure, operations, and practices.

For grade GS-7 Insurance Examiner, the experience must provide knowledge of the insurance practices, programs and requirements.

For grade GS-7 Loan Specialist, the experience must provide knowledge of loans, loan requirements, and a type of loan (e.g., realty, commercial).

• Industrial Property Management

The education must be in one of the following fields: Accounting, Business Administration, Industrial or Production Management, Law, Marketing, Statistics, or related fields.

The experience must be related to general business and/or industrial practices. For grade GS-7 positions, the experience must involve work related to personal 'or industrial property, knowledge of contracts, and government sales contracts.

• Industrial Specialist

The education must be in one of the following fields: Applied Sciences (e.g., Chemistry), Business Administration, Engineering, Industrial Management, or related fields.

The experience must be related to industrial production operations.

For grade GS-7 positions, the experience must be directly related to industrial production operations, practices, methods, materials, etc.

• Quality Assurance Specialist

The education must be in one of the following fields: Computer Science, Engineering or Engineering Technology, Production Management (Business Administration), Mathematics, Physical Sciences (e.g., Chemistry, Physics), Quality Assurance, Statistics, Textiles, or related fields.

The experience must be related to quality control or inspection, contracts and purchasing, engineering, or testing.

For grade GS-7 positions, the experience must be related to maintaining or controlling the quality of products or services.

• Trade Specialist

The education must be in one of the following fields: Business Administration, Business or Commercial Law, Economics, Finance, History, International Relations, International Trade, Marketing, Political Science, or Public Administration.

The experience must be related to the distribution of goods and services (e.g., merchandising, market research).

For grade GS-7 positions, the experience must directly involve marketing and business practices related to distribution.

- **Traffic Management, Transportation Industry Analysis, Transportation Operations, Transportation Specialist and Highway Safety Management**

The education must be in one of the following fields: Accounting, Business Administration, Business or Commercial Law, Commerce, Economics, Engineering, Finance, Motor Mechanics, Industrial Management, Statistics, Traffic Management, Transportation, or related fields. Public Administration and Hazardous Materials Management and qualifying for Highway Safety Management.

The experience must be related to traffic or transportation programs or operations.

For Transportation Industry Analysis the experience must also relate to the business practices and market structures and trends of commercial organizations.

For grade GS-7 positions, the experience must be directly related to the transportation field, management, or operations.

Alternate requirements: Being a certified member of the American Society of Traffic and Transportation meets the requirements for grade GS-5 positions.

- **Unemployment Insurance**
The education must be in one of the following fields: Business Administration, Economics, Industrial Relations, Law, Political Science, Public Administration, Sociology, or Mathematics or Statistics as applied to these fields.

The experience must be in or related to a social science field (e.g., economics, sociology).

For grade GS-7 positions, the experience must be directly related to social insurance.

Related Qualifications Information

- **Students**
Applications will be accepted from students who expect to complete, within the next nine months, courses which would qualify them for the positions for which they are applying.

- **Verification of College Coursework**
You will be required to furnish proof of claimed scholastic achievement at the time of selection.

- **Combining Education and Experience**
You may combine education and experience to meet the qualification requirements. One academic year of full-time study (30 semester hours or 45 quarter hours) is equivalent to 9 months of responsible experience. A bachelor's degree is equivalent to 3 years of responsible experience.

- **Responsible Experience**
To be considered as qualifying experience for these positions, your experience must include all of the following:
    —Analyzing problems and presenting solutions;
    —Planning and organizing work;
    —Communicating verbally and in writing.

- **Nonaccredited College Coursework**
Successful completion of college study in nonaccredited institutions will be accepted to the extent that (1) the courses are accepted for advanced credit at an accredited institution; or (2) the institution is one whose transcript is given full credit by a State University; or (3) the courses have been evaluated and ap-

(Continued on next page)

Instructions for Completing Test Scheduling Card, OPM Form 5000AB

1. Items 1 and 3 are completed with the appropriate responses for this examination. All other items are self explanatory.
2. When completing the form, be sure that the second copy is directly under the first. A "carbon copy" will be made on the second copy.
3. Separate **completed** Test Scheduling Cards along perforation on top of card. Mail both copies to the OPM office which covers the location where you wish to be tested. See page 6 for list of OPM offices and addresses.

TEST SCHEDULING CARD

| 1. Title of Examination **BUSINESS, FINANCE and MANAGEMENT** | 2. Social Security Number | 3. Announcement No. **0001B** |

| 4. Birth Date *(Month, day, year)* | 5. Telephone Number *(Include Area Code)* | 6. Where do you wish to take written test? City: State: |

| 7. If you have performed active duty in the armed forces of the United States and were separated under honorable conditions, indicate periods of service: From: *(Month, day, year)*   To: *(Month, day, year)* | 8. ☐ Check here if you observe the Sabbath or religious holiday on a day other than Sunday (specify day) or have a disability that will require special or individual testing arrangement. Specify the nature and degree of your disability and the special arrangements you will need. |

9. Do you you claim veteran preference? ☐ No ☐ Yes If yes, based on:
☐ (1) Active duty in the armed forces of the U.S. during the period December 7, 1941, through July 1, 1955; (2) more than 180 consecutive days of active duty (other than for training) in the armed forces of the U.S., any part of which occurred after January 31, 1955, and before October 15, 1976; or (3) after service in a campaign for which a campaign badge has been authorized.
☐ Your status as: (1) a disabled veteran or a veteran who was awarded the Purple Heart for wounds or injuries received in action; (2) a spouse of deceased veteran who has not remarried; (3) the spouse of a veteran who has a service-connected disability which disqualifies the veteran for civil service appointment; or (4) the widowed, divorced or separated mother of an ex-service son or daughter who died in action or who is totally and permanently disabled.

10. Are you a United States citizen? ☐ Yes ☐ No

DO NOT WRITE IN THIS SPACE

Give Address Where You Wish to Be Notified of Time and Place for Examination

CHECK COPY TO BE SURE IT IS LEGIBLE	Name *(First, middle, last)*
	Address *(Number and street, R.D., or post office box number)*
	City, State and ZIP Code *(ZIP Code must be included)*

This card will be returned to you.
Bring it with you when you report for the written test.

| **ADMISSION NOTICE** | **IDENTIFICATION MAY BE REQUIRED FOR WRITTEN EXAMINATIONS** *The Federal Government Is an Equal Opportunity Employer* | OPM Form 5000-A (Rev. 10/80) |

TYPE OR PRINT IN INK

4

proved by a State department of education; or (4) the coursework has been evaluated by an organization recognized for accreditation by the Council on Postsecondary Accreditation.

Application Procedures

There are two basic ways to apply for positions: (I) you may take a written test, or (II) you may apply based on your scholastic achievement.

I. Written Test

About the Test

In addition to meeting the qualification requirements, a written test is required to receive consideration on an OPM list of eligibles. This list of eligibles is used by agencies to fill vacancies. Tests are conducted in various locations. The written test consists of two parts. The first part measures your ability to do the jobs for which you are applying. The second part of the test, the Individual Achievement Record (IAR), evaluates how well you have used the opportunities you have had in school, work, or outside activities. You must receive a score of 70 or above to be eligible.

Applicants who have received an eligible rating in the last 12 months for this examination are restricted from taking the written test.

How to Apply for the Written Test

To apply to take the written test, complete the *Test Scheduling Card*, OPM Form 5000AB, printed at bottom of page one of this pamphlet and mail both copies to the OPM office which covers the location where you want to be tested (see the attached list of offices).

You will be notified when and where to take the written test, and will be provided the necessary application forms and sample questions. You must bring the completed forms with you to the written test.

Bilingual/Bicultural Program

Applicants who have Spanish language proficiency or knowledge of Hispanic culture and who pass the written tests may be hired

directly by agencies for positions which require such knowledge or ability. Consideration under this provision would require applying directly to agencies once you have passed the written test and obtained an eligible Notice of Rating. This provision is based on a court order and is separate from consideration on a list of eligibles.

II. Application Based on Scholastic Achievement

Direct Application to Agencies

You may apply directly to agencies for employment consideration if you meet the Outstanding Scholar Provisions identified below. These provisions are based on a court order and are separate from consideration on OPM's list of eligibles.

To qualify for consideration under the Outstanding Scholar Provisions, you must be a college graduate and have a grade-point average (GPA) of 3.5 or above, on a 4.0 scale, for all undergraduate course work, or have graduated in the upper ten (10) percent of your class. Your GPA can be rounded in the following manner: a 3.44 is rounded down to 3.4; a 3.45 is rounded up to 3.5.

Referral by OPM

You may receive additional consideration if you meet either of the above Outstanding Scholar Provisions. Applicants who meet these provisions can be on an OPM referral list which will be an option that Federal agencies can use to fill positions. *Agencies are not required to request a referral list to fill their positions; use of these lists is optional.*

How to Apply for Referral by OPM

Submit a completed Administrative Careers with America Referral Form, OPM Form 1203AS, to: Office of Personnel Management, Staffing Service Center, Examining Office, P.O. Box 9035, Macon, GA 31297-6899. The Form may be obtained from

(Continued on next page)

any of the OPM offices listed on the last page or by calling the College Hotline on 900-990-9200. There is a $.40-a-minute charge for this service.

Note: You do not need to submit a Standard Form (SF) 171, *Application for Federal Employment,* to OPM. However, an agency may require an SF 171 when they consider you for employment.

Special Notes

• Persons With Disabilities
If you have a disability that requires special testing arrangements, please indicate the nature of your disability on the *Test Scheduling Card* (OPM Form 5000AB) so that the appropriate testing arrangements may be made.

• Notice of Results
You will receive a written notice of results which shows your rating within 4 weeks after you take the written test or submit an application based on the Outstanding Scholar Provisions.

• Consideration for Employment
Eligible candidates are referred from OPM registers (lists of eligible candidates) to Federal agencies for employment consideration in score order. You will receive consideration without regard to race, religion, color, national origin, sex, politics, or age.

• Ten-Point Veteran Preference
Ten-point preference is awarded to disabled veterans and mothers, widows or widowers, and spouses of disabled or deceased veterans. You must include a *Claim for 10-Point Veteran Preference,* Standard Form 15, and supporting documentation if you are claiming ten-point preference.

• Citizenship
The positions covered by this examination are included in the Federal competitive service and therefore are open only to citizens of the United States and natives of American Samoa.

• Selective Service Registration
If you are a male born after December 31, 1959, you must be registered with the Selective Service System or have a valid exemption in order to be eligible for Federal employment. You will be required to certify as to your status at the time of appointment.

• Salaries
Federal salary levels are reviewed and adjusted at regular intervals. Current salary rates can be obtained at Federal Job Information Centers.

Areas Not Covered

The list of eligible candidates resulting from this examination will not be used to fill positions in Alaska, Hawaii and Pacific overseas, and Puerto Rico and U.S. Virgin Islands. For information contact the following offices:

• Positions in Alaska:
Office of Personnel Management
Anchorage Area Office
Federal Building
222 W. 7th Ave. #22
Anchorage, AK 99513-7572

• Positions in Hawaii and Pacific Overseas:
Office of Personnel Management
Honolulu Area Office
Federal Building, Room 5316
300 Ala Moana Blvd.
Honolulu, HI 96850

• Positions in Puerto Rico and U.S. Virgin Islands
Office of Personnel Management
San Juan Area Office
Federico Degetau Federal Building
Carlos E. Chardon St.
Hato Rey, PR 00918

Further Information

To obtain information on these and other occupations, you should contact the nearest OPM office (see the attached list), or call the Federal College Hotline on 900-990-9200.

IMPORTANT DO *NOT* COMPLETE THE FORM BELOW. It will be duplicated when you complete the form on page three.

TEST SCHEDULING CARD

1. Title of Examination **BUSINESS, FINANCE and MANAGEMENT**	2. Social Security Number	3. Announcement No. **0001B**

4. Birth Date *(Month, day, year)*	5. Telephone Number *(Include Area Code)*	6. Where do you wish to take written test? City: State:

7. If you have performed active duty in the armed forces of the United States and were separated under honorable conditions, indicate periods of service:
From: *(Month, day, year)*   To: *(Month, day, year)*

8. ☐ Check here if you observe the Sabbath or religious holiday on a day other than Sunday (specify day) or have a disability that will require special or individual testing arrangement. Specify the nature and degree of your disability and the special arrangements you will need.

9. Do you you claim veteran preference? ☐ No ☐ Yes If yes, based on:
☐ (1) Active duty in the armed forces of the U.S. during the period December 7, 1941, through July 1, 1955; (2) more than 180 consecutive days of active duty (other than for training) in the armed forces of the U.S., any part of which occurred after January 31, 1955, and before October 15, 1976; or (3) after service in a campaign for which a campaign badge has been authorized.
☐ Your status as: (1) a disabled veteran or a veteran who was awarded the Purple Heart for wounds or injuries received in action; (2) a spouse of deceased veteran who has not remarried; (3) the spouse of a veteran who has a service-connected disability which disqualifies the veteran for civil service appointment; or (4) the widowed, divorced or separated mother of an ex-service son or daughter who died in action or who is totally and permanently disabled.

10. Are you a United States citizen? ☐ Yes ☐ No

DO NOT WRITE IN THIS SPACE

Give Address Where You Wish to Be Notified of Time and Place for Examination

CHECK COPY TO BE SURE IT IS LEGIBLE	Name *(First, middle, last)*
	Address *(Number and street, R.D., or post office box number)*
	City, State and ZIP Code *(ZIP Code must be included)*

This card will be returned to you.
Bring it with you when you report for the written test.

RECORD CARD IDENTIFICATION MAY BE REQUIRED FOR WRITTEN EXAMINATIONS
The Federal Government Is an Equal Opportunity Employer

OPM Form 5000-A
(Rev. 10/80)

Office of Personnel Management
Where to File to Take a Test

Send your *Test Scheduling Card,* OPM Form 5000AB, to the office listed for the area where you would like to be tested. Offices will schedule you for testing in the location you request if at all possible. Otherwise, you will be scheduled in the closest location where tests are given. You will be contacted concerning the time and location of the test, and provided the necessary forms to bring to the test.

ALABAMA
Huntsville:
Building 600, Suite 341
3322 Memorial Pkwy., South
35801-5311

ALASKA
Anchorage:
Federal Building, Box 22
222 W. 7th Ave., 99513

ARIZONA
Phoenix:
3225 N. Central Avenue
Rm. 1415, 85012

ARKANSAS
(See address for Oklahoma listing)

CALIFORNIA
Los Angeles (For Southern California):
Linder Building, 3rd Floor
845 S. Figueroa, 90017

Sacramento (For Northern California):
1029 J St., 2nd Floor, 95814

San Diego (For San Diego area):
Federal Building, Rm. 4-S-9
880 Front St., 92188

San Francisco (For Central California):
P.O. Box 7405, 94120
(Located at 211 Main St.,
2nd Floor, Room 235)

COLORADO
Denver:
P.O. Box 25167, 80225
(Located at: 12345 W. Alameda Pkwy.
Lakewood, CO)

CONNECTICUT
Hartford:
Federal Building, Rm. 613
450 Main St., 06103

DELAWARE
(See address for Pennsylvania/
Philadelphia listing)

DISTRICT OF COLUMBIA
Metro Area:
1900 E St., N.W., Rm. 1416
Washington, DC 20415-0001
(See Virginia and Maryland state listings
for locations in those states covered.)

FLORIDA
Orlando:
Commodore Building, Ste 150
3444 McCrory Pl., 32803-3701

GEORGIA
Atlanta:
Richard B. Russell Fed. Bldg., Rm. 960
75 Spring St., S.W., 30303

HAWAII
Honolulu (and other Hawaiian Islands
and overseas):
Federal Building, Rm. 5316
300 Ala Moana Blvd., 96850

IDAHO
(See address for Washington listing)

ILLINOIS
Chicago:
175 W. Jackson Blvd., Rm. 530, 60604
(For Madison and St. Clair Counties
see address for Missouri/St. Louis
listing.)

INDIANA
Indianapolis:
Minton-Capehart Federal Building
575 N. Pennsylvania St., 46204

IOWA
(See address for Missouri/Kansas City
listing; for Scott County see address for
Illinois listing; for Pottawattamie County
see address for Kansas listing.)

KANSAS
Wichita:
One-Twenty Building, Rm. 101
120 S. Market St., 67202
(For Johnson, Leavenworth and
Wyandotte Counties see address for
Missouri/Kansas City listing.)

KENTUCKY
(See address for Ohio listing; for
Henderson County see address for
Indiana listing.)

LOUISIANA
New Orleans:
1515 Poydras St., Suite 608, 70112

MAINE
(See address for New Hampshire listing)

MARYLAND
Baltimore:
Garmatz Federal Building
101 W. Lombard Street, 21201
(For Charles, Montgomery, and Prince
George's Counties see address for
District of Columbia listing.)

MASSACHUSETTS
Boston:
Thos. P. O'Neill Federal Bldg.,
10 Causeway St., 02222-1031
(For Barnstable, Berkshire, Bristol,
Dukes, Franklin, Hampden, Hampshire,
and Nantucket Counties see address
for Connecticut listing.)

MICHIGAN
Detroit:
477 Michigan Ave., Rm. 565, 48226

MINNESOTA
Twin Cities:
Federal Building
Ft. Snelling, Twin Cities, 55111

MISSISSIPPI
(See address for Alabama listing)

MISSOURI
Kansas City (For Western Missouri):
Federal Building, Rm. 134
601 E. 12th St., 64106

St. Louis (For Eastern Missouri):
Old Post Office Bldg., Rm. 400
815 Olive St., 63101

MONTANA
(See address for Colorado listing)

NEBRASKA
(See address for Kansas listing)

NEVADA
(See address for California/Sacramento
listing)

NEW HAMPSHIRE
Portsmouth:
Thomas J. McIntyre Fed. Bldg., Rm. 104
80 Daniel Street, 03801-3879

NEW JERSEY
Newark:
Peter W. Rodino, Jr., Federal Building
970 Broad Street, 07102
(For Camden County see address for
Pennsylvania/Philadelphia listing.)

NEW MEXICO
Albuquerque:
Federal Building
421 Gold Avenue., S.W., 87102

NEW YORK
New York City, and Nassau, Suffolk,
Westchester, Putnam, Rockland, Dutch-
ess, and Orange counties.
Jacob K. Javits Federal Building
26 Federal Plaza, 10278

Syracuse (All other locations):
James M. Hanley Federal Building
100 S. Clinton St., 13260

NORTH CAROLINA
Raleigh:
P.O. Box 25069
4505 Falls of the Neuse Rd,
Suite 445, 27611-5069

NORTH DAKOTA
(See address for Minnesota listing)

OHIO
Dayton:
Federal Building, Rm. 506
200 W. 2nd St., 45402
(For Van Wert, Auglaize, Hardin,
Marion, Crawford, Richland, Ashland,
Wayne, Stark, Carroll, Columbiana
Counties and all counties *north* of these
see address for Michigan listing.)

OKLAHOMA
Oklahoma City:
200 N.W. Fifth St., 2nd Floor, 73102

OREGON
Portland:
Federal Building, Rm. 376
1220 S.W. Third Ave., 97204

PENNSYLVANIA
Harrisburg (For Central Pennsylvania):
Federal Building, Rm. 168
P.O. Box 761, 17108

Philadelphia (For Eastern Pennsylvania):
Wm. J. Green, Jr., Federal Building
600 Arch St., 19106

Pittsburgh (For Western Pennsylvania):
Federal Building
1000 Liberty Ave., Rm. 119. 15222

PUERTO RICO
San Juan:
Federico Degetau Federal Building
Carlos E. Chardon St.
Hato Rey, P.R. 00918

RHODE ISLAND
(See address for Connecticut listing)

SOUTH CAROLINA
(See address for North Carolina listing)

SOUTH DAKOTA
(See address for Minnesota listing)

TENNESSEE
Memphis:
200 Jefferson Avenue,
Suite 1312, 38103-2335

TEXAS
Dallas: (for North Texas):
1100 Commerce St., Rm. 6B12, 75242

San Antonio: (for South Texas):
8610 Broadway, Rm. 305, 78217

UTAH
(See address for Colorado listing)

VERMONT
(See address for New Hampshire listing)

VIRGINIA
Norfolk:
Federal Building, Rm. 220
200 Granby St., 23510-1886
(For Arlington, Fairfax, Prince William,
King George, Stafford, and Loudoun
Counties, and the cities of Alexandria,
Falls Church, and Fairfax see address
for District of Columbia listing.)

WASHINGTON
Seattle:
Federal Building
915 Second Ave., 98174

WEST VIRGINIA
(See address for Ohio listing)

WISCONSIN
(See address for Minnesota listing; for
Dane, Grant, Green, Iowa, Jefferson,
Kenosha, Lafayette, Milwaukee, Racine,
Rock, Walworth, and Waukesha coun-
ties, see address for Illinois listing.)

WYOMING
(See address for Colorado listing)

INSTITUTIONAL NOMINATION FORM

Form Approved:
OMB No. 3206-0082

The Presidential Management Intern Program

Important Note: This form must be completed for each nominee and attached to the student's Application Form.

1. Name of Nominee

I certify that the above-named student, an applicant for the Presidential Management Intern Program, is a student in good standing of this university, that this person has shown a clear interest in and a commitment to a career in the public service, is currently enrolled and is expected to receive an advanced degree during the current academic year. Furthermore, I certify that this student has been selected using competitive nomination procedures and has demonstrated academic excellence, sound judgment, capacity for leadership, and potential for future professional growth and development. Finally, I certify that this individual is one of the very best students in this university program and upon completion of this program, will fully meet all the criteria to be a nominee for the Presidential Management Intern Program.

2. Full Name of Dean or Department Chairperson Making This Nomination	3. Name and Address of Academic Institution	
4. Title	5. Name of Graduate School or Program	
6. Signature of Nominating Official	7. Date (*month, day, year*)	8. Office Phone Number (*including area code*)

9. Why was this individual selected as a PMI nominee? What criteria were used for nominee selection and how does this candidate meet them?

10. What do you see as this student's greatest growth or improvement during the period of his/her graduate education? What, if any. are the student's weaknesses?

11. Please supply a brief narrative citing specific examples of the student's strengths in the areas of intellectual ability; judgment; leadership and willingness to assume responsibility; ability to work effectively with others; commitment to public program analysis or management as a career; and personal initiative, such as that demonstrated in overcoming social/economic barriers in achieving education.

PMI SURVEY FORM

The Presidential Management Intern Program

Name (Last, First, Middle Initial)	Social Security Number (SSN)

Important Information

You are requested to complete this form. The data you supply will be used for statistical analysis only. Submission of this information is voluntary. Your failure to do so will have no effect on the processing of your application. This form is authorized for use by the Office of Personnel Management ONLY. This form will be separated from all other application materials at Educational Testing Service prior to any screening or evaluation of individual nominees. This information will not be transmitted to OPM until after the screening and selection phases of the PMI process have been completed.

Your Social Security Number (SSN) is requested under the authority of Executive Order 9397 (November 22, 1943) for the orderly administration of personnel records.

Public burden reporting for this collection of information is estimated to take approximately two minutes per response, including time for reviewing instructions, searching existing data sources, and completing and reviewing the collection of information. Send comments regarding the burden estimates or any other aspect of this collection of information, including suggestions for reducing this burden, to U.S. Office of Personnel Management, Reports and Forms Officer, Rm. 500, Court House Square, 2300 Clarendon Blvd., Arlington, VA 22201.

Race and/or National Origin

The categories below provide descriptions of race and national origins. Read the Definition of Category descriptions and then check the box next to the category with which you identify yourself. If you are of mixed race and/or national origin, select the category with which you most closely identify yourself. NOTE: Please mark only ONE box!

Name of Category	Definition of Category
☐ A. American Indian or Alaskan Native	A person having origins in any of the original peoples of North America, and who maintains cultural identification through community recognition or tribal affiliation.
☐ B. Asian or Pacific Islander	A person having origins in any of the original peoples of the Far East, Southeast Asia, the Indian subcontinent, or the Pacific Islands. For example, this area includes China, India, Japan, Korea, the Philippine Islands and Samoa.
☐ C. Black, not of Hispanic origin	A person having origins in any of the Black racial groups of Africa. This does not include persons of Mexican, Puerto Rican, Cuban, Central or South American, or other Spanish cultures or origins.
☐ D. Hispanic	A person of Mexican, Puerto Rican, Cuban, Central or South American, or other Spanish cultures or origins.
☐ E. White, not of Hispanic origin	A person having origins in any of the original peoples of Europe, North America, or the Middle East. This does not include persons of Mexican, Puerto Rican, Cuban, Central or South American, or other Spanish cultures or origins.
☐ F. Other	A person not included in another category.

PMI Form 001
(6/91)

APPLICATION INSTRUCTIONS
Instructions for Completing Pages 1 and 2

Please use **typewriter** and make sure that entries are readable on the two copies you submit with the original. Use only capital letters on page one of the application. If there is insufficient space to complete an item, enter only as many letters as boxes provided.

Read the instructions for each item **before** completing the data entry boxes for that particular item.

ITEM INSTRUCTIONS

1. **Social Security Number:** Self-explanatory.
2. **Title:** Enter either Ø1 (Mr., Br.) or Ø2 (Ms, Miss, Mrs., Sr.).
3-5. **Name (Last, First, Middle Initial):** Self-explanatory.
6. **Legal Residence:** Enter one of the following two-letter abbreviations.

AL Alabama	GA Georgia	MD Maryland	NM New Mexico	SD South Dakota
AK Alaska	GU Guam	MA Massachusetts	NY New York	TN Tennessee
AZ Arizona	HI Hawaii	MI Michigan	NC North Carolina	TX Texas
AR Arkansas	ID Idaho	MN Minnesota	ND North Dakota	UT Utah
CA California	IL Illinois	MS Mississippi	OH Ohio	VT Vermont
CZ Canal Zone	IN Indiana	MO Missouri	OK Oklahoma	VI Virgin Islands
CO Colorado	IA Iowa	MT Montana	OR Oregon	VA Virginia
CT Connecticut	KS Kansas	NE Nebraska	PA Pennsylvania	WA Washington
DE Delaware	KY Kentucky	NV Nevada	PR Puerto Rico	WV West Virginia
DC District of Columbia	LA Louisiana	NH New Hampshire	RI Rhode Island	WI Wisconsin
FL Florida	ME Maine	NJ New Jersey	SC South Carolina	WY Wyoming

7. **State and Local Interest:** Self-explanatory.
8. **Geographic Availability:** Enter the code which best identifies where you will accept a job.
   If you will accept a job in only a specific location (e.g., one city or state), you may write the name of that location in the space following the code boxes. However, you **must also** enter the most appropriate code from the list below.

12—**Anywhere in the U.S.**

11—**Only in the Washington, D.C., Metropolitan Area**

10—**Only in the Seattle Area**
(Alaska, Idaho, Oregon, Washington)

09—**Only in the San Francisco Area**
(Arizona, California, Hawaii, Nevada)

08—**Only in the Denver Area**
(Colorado, Montana, North Dakota, South Dakota, Utah, Wyoming)

07—**Only in the St. Louis Area**
(Iowa, Kansas, Missouri, Nebraska)

06—**Only in the Dallas Area**
(Arkansas, Louisiana, New Mexico, Oklahoma, Texas)

05—**Only in the Chicago Area**
(Illinois, Indiana, Michigan, Minnesota, Ohio, Wisconsin)

04—**Only in the Atlanta Area**
(Alabama, Florida, Georgia, Kentucky, Mississippi, Tennessee, North Carolina, South Carolina)

03—**Only in the Philadelphia Area**
(Delaware, Maryland, Pennsylvania, Virginia, West Virginia

02—**Only in the New York Area**
(New Jersey, New York, Puerto Rico)

01—**Only in the Boston Area**
(Connecticut, Maine, Massachusetts, New Hampshire, Rhode Island, Vermont)

9. **Veterans' Preference:** Enter the number in the box which identifies your veterans' preference. If you are claiming veterans' preference, you must include with your application a copy of your Form DD 214. In addition, if you claim a 10-point preference, please complete and attach Standard Form 15, *"Application for 10-Point Veterans' Preference,"* together with the proof called for in that form.

1	No veterans' preference	4	10-point compensably disabled (30% or more)
2	5-point preference based on active duty in the Armed Forces (if marked, you will be required to support your claim at the time you apply)	5	10-point non-compensably disabled or Purple Heart recipient
		6	10-point spouse
3	10-point compensably disabled (less than 30%)	7	10-point widow(er) or mother

10. **Birthdate:** Enter month, day, year (for example, March 3, 1954, would be entered 030354).

> NOTE: YOU MUST ANSWER QUESTIONS 11 AND 12 FOR YOUR APPLICATION TO RECEIVE ANY CONSIDERATION.
>
> 11. **U.S. Citizenship:** Self-explanatory.
> 12. **Date of Degree:** Enter the month and year you completed or expect to complete your current graduate degree.

13-14. **Home and Other Phones:** Enter the area code and number of your current home phone and of a second phone (e.g., at work, relative's) where you can be contacted or a message can be left.

15-18. **Current Address:** Use standard abbreviations.

19. **Until:** If you anticipate leaving the current address you entered under items 15-18 before next June, enter the approximate month/day/year after which that address will not be valid.
IF YOU DO NOT ANTICIPATE MOVING FROM YOUR CURRENT ADDRESS, LEAVE ITEM 19 BLANK.

20-23. If you entered a moving date in item 19, please provide an alternative address where mail will reach you or will be forwarded to you. IF YOU LEFT ITEM 19 BLANK, DO NOT MAKE ENTRIES IN ITEMS 20-23.

24. **University:** Enter the full name of the university or college, followed by the school or department, from which you are receiving your graduate degree.

DO NOT MARK IN SHADED BOXES.

25. **Graduate Degree:** Enter the code below which most appropriately identifies the graduate degree you are receiving this academic year. If you are receiving a dual degree, enter the code for the one degree you feel is most relevant to this Program; you will have the opportunity to record the second degree under Item 26.
NOTE: THIS LISTING OF GRADUATE DEGREES DOES NOT INDICATE ELIGIBILITY OF A LISTED DEGREE NOR DOES IT IMPLY INELIGIBILITY FOR A DEGREE NOT LISTED.

MASTER'S DEGREE IN:

01	Public or government administration/management	10	Human resources or social administration
02	Public policy	11	Social work
03	Urban, city, and/or regional administration/management	12	Community development
04	Planning	13	Public health or health administration
05	Criminal justice or administration of justice	14	Political or international economics
06	International affairs/administration	15	Educational administration
07	Political science/government	16	Industrial relations
08	Business administration	17	Natural resources
09	Management/administration	18	Technology or engineering
		20	(Master's degree in an area not listed)

DOCTORAL DEGREE IN:

31	Public or government administration/management	35	Business administration
32	Public policy	36	Educational administration
33	Planning	40	(Doctoral degree in an area not listed)
34	Political science/government		

26. **Other Graduate Degree:** Enter the appropriate code indicating any graduate degree, **other than that in Item 25,** that you have received.

1 No other graduate degree	6 Master of management/business administration
2 Master of arts and letters or education	7 Master of public administration/political science/
3 Master of engineering or science discipline	policy studies
4 Master of social or behavioral science	8 JD or other law degree
5 Master of public health or health administration	9 (Master's or Doctoral degree in an area not listed)

27. **Desired Screening Panel Site:** Item 27 lists potential locations for the interview portion of the screening process. Interviews are held during the month of February. Please check the site which will be the most convenient to you during that month. You are responsible for travel expenses to attend the interviews. **We cannot guarantee scheduling at your desired site but we will attempt to schedule you for a panel as close as possible to your indicated location.**

27A. **Enter the dates** during the month of February that you will be available to attend the interview.

28. **Special Physical Arrangements:** Self-explanatory.

29-31. **Academic Experience:** Self-explanatory.

32. **Professional Experience:** Enter the code from the list below which correctly describes the length of your **professional** experience in each of the employment areas.

0 No experience	3 1 to 3 years full-time or its equivalent
1 Less than 6 months full-time or its equivalent	4 3 years or more full-time or its equivalent
2 6 months to 1 year full-time or its equivalent	

33-34. **Knowledge:** Enter the code from the list below which most accurately identifies the area of your greatest public program analysis or management knowledge in: Academic Studies [33], and Applied situations (employed or volunteer) [34]. If you feel that your knowledge is very broad based or is that of a generalist, enter 2195 (Administrative and Management Processes).

2195	Administrative and Management Processes	0798	Quantitative Methods/Information Systems
2197	Policy Analysis	2196	Urban/Intergovernmental Affairs
0597	Individual/Group/Organizational Theory and Dynamics	2210	International Relations
		2105	Criminal Justice Administration
0509	Procurement/Contracts/Grants	1214	Public Health Administration
0515	Personnel/Labor Relations/Employee Development	0206	City/Community/Regional Planning
		2101	Human Resources/Community Service
0598	Finance/Economics/Budgeting/Accounting	0115	Natural Resources/Environment

35. **Applied Knowledge Experience:** Enter the amount of your experience in the Applied area you identified in Item 34. Use the same "length of experience" codes used for Item 32.

Instructions for Completing Pages 3 through 7

Please **type** all responses. Answer all questions completely in the space provided. If additional space is needed, you may attach sheets of paper of the same size as this page. Make sure your name and social security number (SSN) are on any attachments. **Note: No additional sheets of paper will be accepted for questions 40-41 found on pages 6 and 7.** If an item does not apply to you, or if there is no information to be given, please write the letters "N.A." for Not Applicable.

Be sure to sign the certification statement on page 8. You cannot be selected for the Program without a signed Application Form.

APPLICATION FORM

Form Approved
OMB No. 3206-0082

The Presidential Management Intern Program

Important Note: Complete this form only after reading instructions on previous pages.

A. PERSONAL INFORMATION

1. Social Security Number

2. Title

3. Last Name

4. First Name

5. M. I.

6. Legal Residence

7. May we refer your name for possible consideration to: (If "YES," check box(es).)
   - State or Local Governments
   - Other Public Organizations

8. Geographic Availability

9. Veterans' Preference

10. Birthdate (Month, Day Year)

11. Are you a U.S. citizen? (Check one box.)
    - Yes
    - No

12. Date of Degree
    | Month | Year |

13. Home Phone—Include Area Code

14. Other Phone—Include Area Code

15. Current Address (Items 15-18)—Street Number and Name

16. City

17. State

18. Zip Code

19. Until...
    | Month | Day | Year |

20. Address at which mail will always reach you, if different from current address (Items 21-23) Street Number and Name

21. City

22. State

23. Zip Code

24. University/School/Department

25. Graduate Degree

26. Other Graduate Degree

27. Desired Regional Screening Panel Location (See Instructions. Please check only one regional location.)

Atlanta Region
- Atlanta, GA
- Jackson, MS
- Orlando, FL
- Raleigh, NC

Chicago Region
- Chicago, IL
- Dayton, OH
- Detroit, MI
- Indianapolis, IN

- Kansas City, MO
- St. Louis, MO
- Twin Cities, MN
- Witchita, KS

Philadelphia Region
- Boston, MA
- New York, NY
- Philadelphia, PA
- Pittsburgh, PA
- San Juan, Puerto Rico

- Syracuse, NY

San Francisco Region
- Los Angeles, CA
- San Francisco, CA
- Seattle, WA

Dallas Region
- Albuquerque, NM
- Dallas, TX
- Denver, CO

- New Orleans, LA
- Oklahoma City, OK
- Phoenix, AZ
- San Antonio, TX

Washington, DC
- Washington, DC

27A. Availability Dates for Regional Screening Panels.

28. If you will require special physical arrangements or assistance at the regional screening panel, please check this box. You will be contacted and preparations will be made in advance.

OPM Form 1300
Rev. 5/90

110

B. KNOWLEDGE AND EXPERIENCE

29. List each of your graduate level courses in public sector management or public policy analysis under the area heading most appropriate to its primary focus. You may list courses you anticipate taking during the next academic term. List each course title on a separate line or place slash marks between courses. **In the box beside each area heading, enter the _number_ of _graduate courses_ you have taken in that area.** If you have not taken any courses in a given area, enter Ø. If you have taken nine or more courses in an area, enter 9. If selected as a Presidential Management Intern, finalists must verify graduate course work at time of appointment.

COURSES

A. General Administrative and Management Processes

B. Employment/Personnel/Labor Relations

C. Program and Policy Analysis

D. Finance/Budgeting/Economics/Accounting

E. Political Processes

F. Quantitative Methods/Information Systems

G. Individual/Group/Organization - Theory and Dynamics

H. Other

30. Was a public sector internship part of your graduate degree requirements? | YES | NO

31. Give the actual or proposed subject of your thesis, dissertation, or major academic research work.

32. Professional Experience *(See Instructions)*

- Federal *(Non-Military)* *(Includes Federal Government or Congressional Employment)*
- Private Sector *(Includes Self-Employment)*
- State or Local *(Includes State and Local Governments and Intergovernmental Public Agencies)*
- Educational *(Teaching, Graduate Assistantships and Educational Administration)*
- Not-For-Profit *(Organizations or Associations)*
- Armed Services *(Leadership Capacity Only)*

33. Academic Knowledge

34. Applied Knowledge

35. Applied Knowledge Experience

111

C. ACADEMIC BACKGROUND

36. Name and location *(City, State and ZIP Code, if known)* of all colleges or universities attended, beginning with your current school and working back.	Dates Attended		Credits Completed (Semester = S Quarter = Q)	Major Field of Study	Grade Point Average and Base	Degree Title and Year Received. or Month and Year Expected
	From	To				

D. WORK EXPERIENCE

37. In blocks a-d describe in detail your work experience. Please account for **ALL** time over the past 10 years, or since high school, if applicable. Incorporate in your description of duties information about progression in your work assignments; the nature, variety, and complexity of your achievements; the scope and level of your responsibility and your relationship to other factors which help describe your job. Please list your work experience in chronological order, beginning with your most recent job. Do not submit agency or company position descriptions. Describe the experience in your own words.

May inquiry be made of your present employer regarding your character, qualifications, and record of employment? ☐ Yes ☐ No

a. Name and Complete Address of Employer	Dates Employed	Salary or Earnings	Average Hours per Week
	From: To:	Beginning $ Per Ending $ Per	
	If Federal Service, Civilian or Military Series, Grade, or Rank, and Date of Last Promotion	Exact Title of Your Position	
Name and Phone Number of Immediate Supervisor	Number and Kind of Employees You Supervised	Kind of Business or Organization	

Reason for Leaving:

Description of Duties:

b. Name and Complete Address of Employer	Dates Employed	Salary or Earnings	Average Hours per Week
	From: To:	Beginning $ Per Ending $ Per	
	If Federal Service, Civilian or Military Series, Grade, or Rank, and Date of Last Promotion	Exact Title of Your Position	
Name and Phone Number of Immediate Supervisor	Number and Kind of Employees You Supervised	Kind of Business or Organization	

Reason for Leaving:

Description of Duties:

Name *(Last, First, M.I.)*

c.	Name and Complete Address of Employer	Dates Employed	Salary or Earnings	Average Hours per Week
		From: To:	Beginning $ Per Ending $ Per	
		If Federal Service, Civilian or Military Series, Grade, or Rank, and Date of Last Promotion	Exact Title of Your Position	

Name and Phone Number of Immediate Supervisor	Number and Kind of Employees You Supervised	Kind of Business or Organization

Reason for Leaving:

Description of Duties:

d.	Name and Complete Address of Employer	Dates Employed	Salary or Earnings	Average Hours per Week
		From: To:	Beginning $ Per Ending $ Per	
		If Federal Service, Civilian or Military Series, Grade, or Rank, and Date of Last Promotion	Exact Title of Your Position	

Name and Phone Number of Immediate Supervisor	Number and Kind of Employees You Supervised	Kind of Business or Organization

Reason for Leaving:

Description of Duties:

E. ACTIVITIES AND ACHIEVEMENTS

38. List the major college, civic, business, and professional activities in which you have participated during the past five years. Describe the extent, duration, and significance of your involvement. Also, list any awards or special recognition you have received for these activities. Do not list any information that you included under Item 37—Work Experience.

39. List any outstanding accomplishments, such as awards or publications, not mentioned above. Also, list the foreign and/or computer languages of which you have knowledge, and indicate your present level of proficiency—excellent, good, fair.

F. The following questions are designed to give the selection committee a sense of: (1) your professional interest in the Federal service and your motivation for a Presidental Management Internship; and (2) the quality of your thinking and writing about issues of public policy and program management. **The answers to these questions must be typed in the blank space provided after each question (no additional sheets will be accepted).**

40. Explain why you are seeking entry to the Federal service through the PMI Program, describe in what area(s) of public policy or program management your career interests lie and in which Federal agency or agencies you would want to work, if selected.

41. Select and analyze an issue of public policy or program management which is of particular concern to you from those you have identified above. Your discussion should be in the form of a policy recommendation and should include a factual description of the matter at issue, your opinion on it, your recommendations for changes, if any, and the reasons supporting your opinion and recommendations.

Answer Items 42 through 44 by placing an "X" in the proper column.	YES	NO

42. Veterans' Preference

    A. Have you served on active duty in the United States Military Service? If your only active duty was training in the Reserves or National Guard, answer "NO". If "**NO**", go to Item 43 . . . .

    B. Were you honorably discharged from the military service? If your discharge was changed to "honorable" or "general" by a Discharge Review Board, answer "YES". *If you received a clemency discharge, answer "NO". If "NO", explain in Item 45 below . . . .

        *Include the date and type of discharge you received.

Note: A conviction or a firing does not necessarily mean you cannot be appointed.

43. During the last **10 years**, were you **fired from any job** for any reason, did you **quit after being told that you would be fired**, or did you leave by mutual agreement because of specific problems? If "**Yes**", write in Item 45 below for each job: (a) the name and address of the employer; (b) the approximate date you left the job; and (c) the reason(s) why you left.

44. **When answering questions A, B, C, D and E, include convictions resulting from a plea of nolo contendre (no contest). You may omit:** (1) traffic fines of $100.00 or less; (2) any violation of law committed before your 16th birthday; (3) any violation of law committed before your 18th birthday, if finally decided in juvenile court or under a Youth Offender law; (4) any conviction set aside under the Federal Youth Corrections Act or similar State law; (5) any conviction whose record was expunged under Federal or State law.

    A. Have you **ever** been convicted of, or forfeited collateral for **any felony violation**? . . . .

        Generally, a felony is defined as any violation of law punishable by imprisonment of longer than one year, except for violations called misdemeanors under State law which are punishable by imprisonment of two years or less.

    B. Have you **ever** been convicted of or forfeited collateral for any **firearms** or **explosives** violation? . . . .

    C. Are you **now** under charges for **any** violation of law? . . . .

    D. During the last **10 years** have you forfeited collateral, been convicted, been imprisoned, been on probation, or been on parole? Do **not** include violations reported in **A, B,** or **C** above . . . .

    E. Have you **ever** been convicted by a military **court-martial**? If no military service, answer "NO" . . . .

    F. Are you **delinquent** on any Federal debt? *(Include delinquencies arising from Federal taxes, loans, overpayment of benefits, and other debts to the U.S. Government plus defaults on Federally guaranteed or insured loans such as student and home mortgage loans)* . . . .

    IF YOU ANSWERED "YES" TO ANY PART OF ITEM 44 (A-E), GIVE DETAILS IN ITEM 45 BELOW. For each violation write the: (1) date; (2) charge; (3) place; (4) court; and (5) action taken. For question 44 (F), please explain the type, length and amount of the delinquency or default, and steps you are taking to correct errors or repay the debt. Give any identification number associated with the debt and the address of the Federal agency involved.

45. Additional Space for Answers (Write the number to which each answer applies. **If you need more space,** include your name and SSN on attached sheets.

46. Signature, Certification, and Release of Information

    YOU MUST SIGN THIS APPLICATION. Read the following carefully before you sign.

    A false statement on any part of your application may be grounds for not hiring you, or for firing you after you begin work. Also, you may be punished by fine or imprisonment (U.S. Code, Title 18, Section 1001).

    If you are a male born after December 31, 1959, you must be registered with the Selective Service System or have a valid exemption in order to be eligible for Federal employment. You will be required to certify as to your status at the time of appointment.

    I understand that any information I give may be investigated as allowed by law or Presidential order and may be provided to agencies of the Federal Government.

    I consent to the release of information about my ability and fitness for Federal employment by *employers, schools, law enforcement agencies and other individuals or organizations, investigators, personnel staffing specialists, and other authorized employees of the Federal Government.*

    I consent to the release of information about the status of my application to university officials.

    I certify that, to the best of my knowledge and belief, **all** of my statements are true, correct, complete, and made in good faith.

SIGNATURE *(Sign each application in dark ink)*	DATE SIGNED *(Month,. day, year)*

INDEPENDENT EVALUATION

Form Approved:
OMB No. 3306-0082

The Presidential Management Intern Program

APPLICANT: Please print or type your name: _____

The Presidential Management Intern (PMI) Program seeks to attract to the Federal service outstanding men and women from a variety of academic disciplines who have a clear interest in, and commitment to, a career in the analysis and management of public policies and programs.

The above-named individual has been nominated for the PMI Program. A limited number of finalists (approximately 300 in recent years) are selected each year. To assist in the selection of interns, the Office of Personnel Management and the PMI Review Committee would like your evaluation of the nominee's personal characteristics, potential for a career in public program analysis or management, and motivation. On what criteria do your judgments rest? How does this candidate meet them? We urge you to be as candid as possible, citing any particular incidents that illustrate the nominee's maturity, initiative, and potential. Your prompt submission of this form will be most helpful, as the nominee can neither complete his or her application nor be considered without your remarks. You should be aware, however, that this form, including your identity, is subject to release under the Privacy Act and the Freedom of Information Act, and upon request will be shown to the applicant.

Your evaluation will become part of the nominee's confidential file, intended for use by the PMI Review Committee. Please return this form, plus any additional sheets, in a sealed envelope to the nominee, who will submit the sealed envelope as part of the completed application package.

Thank you for your cooperation.

Name (*First, Last, Middle*) | Address (*Street, City, State and ZIP Code*)

Title

Business or Occupation

How long have you known the nominee?

In what capacity have you known the nominee?

Signature | Date Signed

OPM Form 1301-A
Rev. 9/89

INDEPENDENT EVALUATION

Form Approved:
OMB No. 3306-0082

The Presidential Management Intern Program

APPLICANT: Please print or type your name: _____

The Presidential Management Intern (PMI) Program seeks to attract to the Federal service outstanding men and women from a variety of academic disciplines who have a clear interest in, and commitment to, a career in the analysis and management of public policies and programs.

The above-named individual has been nominated for the PMI Program. A limited number of finalists (approximately 300 in recent years) are selected each year. To assist in the selection of interns, the Office of Personnel Management and the PMI Review Committee would like your evaluation of the nominee's personal characteristics, potential for a career in public program analysis or management, and motivation. On what criteria do your judgments rest? How does this candidate meet them? We urge you to be as candid as possible, citing any particular incidents that illustrate the nominee's maturity, initiative, and potential. Your prompt submission of this form will be most helpful, as the nominee can neither complete his or her application nor be considered without your remarks. You should be aware, however, that this form, including your identity, is subject to release under the Privacy Act and the Freedom of Information Act, and upon request will be shown to the applicant.

Your evaluation will become part of the nominee's confidential file, intended for use by the PMI Review Committee. Please return this form, plus any additional sheets, in a sealed envelope to the nominee, who will submit the sealed envelope as part of the completed application package.

Thank you for your cooperation.

Name (*First, Last, Middle*)	Address (*Street, City, State and ZIP Code*)
Title	
Business or Occupation	

How long have you known the nominee?

In what capacity have you known the nominee?

Signature	Date Signed

OPM Form 1301-A
Rev. 9/89

119

APPENDIX 3
FEDERAL JOB INFORMATION CENTERS (FJIC)

ALABAMA
Office of Personnel Management
3322 Memorial Pkwy,
South Building 600, Suite 341
Huntsville, AL 35801-5311
205/544-5802

ALASKA
Office of Personnel Management
222 W. 7th Avenue #22
Anchorage, AK 99513-7572
907/271-5821

ARIZONA
Office of Personnel Management
Century Plaza Bldg., Rm 1415
3225 N. Central Avenue
Phoenix, AZ 85012
602/640-5800

ARKANSAS
See Oklahoma Listing

CALIFORNIA
Office of Personnel Management
9650 Flair Drive, Suite 100A
El Monte, CA 91731
818/575-6510

Federal Job Info Ctr.
1029 "J" Street, Room 202
Sacramento, CA 95818
916/551-1464
*This office also covers NV

Office of Personnel Management
211 Main Street, Rm 235
(Mail) PO Box 7405
San Francisco, CA 94120
415/744-5627

Office of Personnel Management
Federal Bldg., Rm 4-S-9
880 Front Street
San Diego, CA 92188
619/557-6165

COLORADO
Office of Personnel Management
12345 W. Alameda Pkwy
PO Box 25167
Denver, CO 80225
303/969-7050
303/969-7055 (forms)
303/969-7052 MT
303/969-7054 UT & WY
*This office also covers WY, MT, UT

CONNECTICUT
Office of Personnel Management
Federal Building, Rm 613
450 Main Street
Hartford, CT 06103
203/240-3096/3263

DELAWARE
See Philadelphia Listing

DISTRICT OF COLUMBIA
Office of Personnel Management
1900 "E" Street, NW, Rm 1416
Washington, DC 20415
202/606-2700

FLORIDA
Office of Personnel Management
Commodore Building, Suite 125
3444 McCrory Place
Orlando, FL 32803-3701
407/648-6148

GEORGIA
Office of Personnel Management
Federal Building, Rm 940A
75 Spring Street, SW
Atlanta, GA 30303
404/331-4315

GUAM
Pacific News Bldg
238 O'Hara St, Rm 902
Agana, Guam 96910
(011-671) 472-7451

HAWAII
Office of Personnel Management
Federal Bldg., Rm 5316
300 Ala Moana Boulevard
Honolulu, HI 96850
808/541-2791
808/541-2784 Overseas

IDAHO
See Washington Listing

ILLINOIS
Office of Personnel Management
175 W Jackson Blvd, Rm 530
Chicago, IL 60604
312/353-6192
For Madison & St. Clair Counties, see
St. Louis, MO listing

INDIANA
Office of Personnel Management
Minton-Capehart Federal Building
575 N Pennsylvania Street
Indianapolis, IN 46204
317/226-7161

IOWA
See Missouri Listing

KANSAS
Office of Personnel Management
120 S. Market Street, Rm 101
Wichita, KS 67202
316/269-6794
In Johnson, Leavenworth &
Wyandotte Counties see Kansas City,
MO listing

KENTUCKY
See Ohio Listing
In Henderson County, see Indiana
listing

LOUISIANA
Office of Personnel Management
1515 Poydras St., Suite 608
New Orleans, LA 70112
504/589-2764

MAINE
See New Hampshire Listing

MARYLAND
Office of Personnel Management
Garmatz Federal Building
101 W. Lombard Street
Baltimore, MD 21201
301/962-3822

MASSACHUSETTS
Office of Personnel Management
Boston Federal Building
10 Causeway Street
Boston, MA 02222
617/565-5900

MICHIGAN
Office of Personnel Management
477 Michigan Avenue, Rm 565
Detroit, MI 48226
313/226-6950

MINNESOTA
Office of Personnel Management
Federal Building Ft Snelling
Twin Cities, MN 55111
612/725-3430
*This office also covers ND,SD

MISSISSIPPI
See Alabama Listing

MISSOURI
Office of Personnel Management
Federal Building, Rm 134
601 E 12th Street
Kansas City, MO 64106
816/426-5702

Office of Personnel Management
Old Post Office Building, Room 134
815 Olive Street
St. Louis, MO 63101
314/539-2285

MONTANA
See Colorado Listing

NEBRASKA
See Kansas Listing

NEVADA
See Sacramento, CA Listing

NEW HAMPSHIRE
Office of Personnel Management
Federal Buiding, Rm 104
80 Daniel Street
Portsmouth, NH 03801
603/431-7115
*This office also covers ME & VT

NEW JERSEY
Office of Personnel Management
Federal Building
970 Broad Street
Newark, NJ 07102
201/645-3673
In Camden, 215/597-7440

NEW MEXICO
Office of Personnel Management
Federal Building
421 Gold Avenue, SW
Albuquerque, NM 87102
505/766-2906

NEW YORK
Office of Personnel Management
Federal Building
26 Federal Plaza
New York, NY 10278
212/264-0422/0423

Office of Personnel Management
James M Hanley Fed Bldg
100 S Clinton Street
Syracuse, NY 13260
315/423-5660

NORTH CAROLINA
Office of Personnel Management
4565 Falls of the Neuse
Road, Suite 4445
Raleigh, NC 27609
919/856-4361

NORTH DAKOTA
See Minnesota Listing

OHIO
Office of Personnel Management
Federal Building, Rm 506
200 W. Second Street
Dayton, OH 45402
513/225-2720
*This office also covers KY, WV

OKLAHOMA
Office of Personnel Management
200 NW 5th Street, 2nd floor
Oklahoma, City OK 73102
405/231-4948
(Mail or phone only)

OREGON
Office of Personnel Management
1220 SW Third Street, Rm 376
Portland, OR 97204
503/326-3141

PENNSYLVANIA
Office of Personnel Management
Federal Building, Rm 168
PO Box 761
Harrisburg, PA 17108
717/782-4494

Office of Personnel Management
William J. Green, Jr Fed Bldg
600 Arch Street, Rm 1416
Philadelphia, PA 19106
215/597-7440
*This office also covers DE

Office of Personnel Management
1000 Liberty Avenue, Fed Bldg
Room 119
Pittsburgh, PA 15222
412/644-2755

PUERTO RICO
Office of Personnel Management
Carlos E. Chardon Street
Hato Rey, PR 00918
809/766-5242

RHODE ISLAND
Office of Personnel Management
Federal & PO Building, Rm 310
Kennedy Plaza
Providence, RI 02903
401/528-5251

SOUTH CAROLINA
See North Carolina Listing

SOUTH DAKOTA
See Minnesota Listing

TENNESSEE
Office of Personnel Management
200 Jefferson Avenue, Suite 1312
(Walk in Only)
Memphis, TN 38103
For mail or phone see AL listing

TEXAS
Office of Personnel Management 1100
Commerce Street, Rm 6B12
Dallas, TX 75242
214/767-8035
(Mail or phone only)

Houston 713/226-2375

Office of Personnel Management
8610 Broadway, Room 305
San Antonio, TX 78217
512/229-6611/6600

UTAH
See Colorado Listing

VERMONT
See New Hampshire Listing

VIRGINIA
Office of Personnel Management
Federal Building, Rm 220
Granby Street
Norfolk, VA 23510
804/441-3355

WASHINGTON
Office of Personnel Management
Seattle Area Office
915 Second Avenue
Seattle, WA 98174
206/442-4365
*This office also covers ID

WEST VIRGINIA
See Ohio Listing

WISCONSIN
312/353-6189
Residents in Grant, Iowa, Lafayette,
Dane, Green, Rock, Jefferson,
Walworth, Waukesha, Racine,
Kenosha & Milwaukee

All other WI residents refer to MN
listing

WYOMING
See Colorado Listing

GENERAL SCHEDULE (GS) SALARY INFORMATION

(RATE STEPS WITHIN EACH GRADE)

GS	ONE	TWO	THREE	FOUR	FIVE	SIX	SEVEN	EIGHT	NINE	TEN
1	11,478	11,861	12,242	12,623	13,006	13,230	13,606	13,986	14,003	14,356
2	12,905	13,212	13,640	14,003	14,157	14,573	14,989	15,405	15,821	16,237
3	14,082	14,551	15,020	15,489	15,958	16,427	16,896	17,365	17,834	18,303
4	15,808	16,335	16,862	17,389	17,916	18,443	18,970	19,497	20,024	20,551
5	17,686	18,276	18,866	19,456	20,046	20,636	21,226	21,816	22,406	22,996
6	19,713	20,370	21,027	21,684	22,341	22,998	23,655	24,312	24,969	25,626
7	21,906	22,636	23,366	24,096	24,826	25,556	26,286	27,016	27,746	28,476
8	24,262	25,071	25,880	26,689	27,498	28,307	29,116	29,925	30,734	31,543
9	26,798	27,691	28,584	29,477	30,370	31,263	32,156	33,049	33,942	34,835
10	29,511	30,495	31,479	32,463	33,447	34,431	35,415	36,399	37,383	38,367
11	32,423	33,504	34,585	35,666	36,747	37,828	38,909	39,990	41,071	42,152
12	38,861	40,156	41,451	42,746	44,041	45,336	46,631	47,926	49,221	50,516
13	46,210	47,750	49,290	50,830	52,370	53,910	55,450	56,990	58,530	60,070
14	54,607	56,427	58,247	60,067	61,887	63,707	65,527	67,347	69,167	70,987
15	64,233	66,374	68,515	70,656	72,797	74,938	77,079	79,220	81,361	83,502

* General Schedule employees in New York, San Francisco and Los Angeles areas receive an additional 8% of basic pay.

127

APPENDIX 5

STATE PERSONNEL OFFICES
AND
STATE JOB INFORMATION CENTERS

ALABAMA
649 Monroe St., Rm 261
Montgomery, AL 36130
205/242-8011

PO Box 20025
Montgomery, AL 20025
205/286-3700

ALASKA
1111 W. 8th
PO Box 3-7000
Juneau, AK 99802
907/465-4531

1002 Glacier Highway
Suite 200
Juneau, AK 99801
907/790-4562

ARIZONA
PO Box 6123
Phoenix, AZ 85005
602/542-6314

397 Malpais Lane,
Suite 9
Flastaff, AZ 86001
602/779-4513

ARKANSAS
PO Box 2981
Little Rock, AR 72203
501/682-2121

PO Box 1205
Fayetteville, AR 72702
501/521-5730

CALIFORNIA
800 Capitol Mall
Sacramento, CA 95814
916/324-5966

396 S. Los Angeles Street
Los Angeles, CA 90013
213/744-2095

COLORADO
600 Grant Street,
Suite 900
Denver, CO 80203
303/837-3902

2555 Airport Road
Colorado Springs, CO 80910
719/634-7766

CONNECTICUT
200 Folly Brook Blvd.
Wethersfield, CT 06109
203/566-5030

90 Washington Street
Hartford, CT 06106
203/566-7682

DELAWARE
PO Box 9499
Newark, DE 19714
302/368-6897

PO Box 616
Dover, DE 19903
302/739-5473

DISTRICT OF COLUMBIA
500 C Street NW
Washington, DC 20001
202/724-3785

25 K Street NE
Washington, DC 20002
202/724-3785

HAWAII
830 Punchbowl St, Rm 421
Honolulu HI 96813
808/548-6468

45-1141 Kemehameha Hwy
Kaneohe, HI 96744
808/235-2111

IDAHO
317 Main Street
Boise, ID 83735
208/334-6142

150 Shoup Ave., Ste 13
Idaho Falls, ID 83402
208/525-7000

ILLINOIS
401 S. State Street #3-5
Chicago, IL 60605
312/793-6822

PO Box 5657
Springfield, IL 62705
217/524-7839

INDIANA
10 N. Senate Avenue,
Room 313
Indianapolis, IN 46204
317/232-0173

160 S. 3rd Avenue
PO Box 10008
Evansville, IN 47708
812/428-2959

IOWA
1000 E. Grand Avenue
Des Moines, IA 50319
515/281-5854

800 7th Street SE
Cedar Rapids, IA 52406
319/365-9474

KANSAS
401 Topeka Blvd.
Topeka, KS 66603
913/296-2524

402 E. 2nd Street
PO Box 877
Wichita, KS 67201
316/266-8600

KENTUCKY
275 E. Main, 2nd Floor
Frankfort, KY 40621
502/564-7456

320 Garrard Street
Covington, KY 41011
606/292-6666

MASSACHUSETTS
1 Knotty Walk
Taunton, MA   02780
508/880-0054

Hurley Bldg., 1st Floor
Boston, MA   02114
617/727-1330

MICHIGAN
7310 Woodward Avenue
Room 417
Detroit, MI   48202
313/876-5361

5015 South Cedar
Lansing, MI   48910
517/334-6729

MINNESOTA
390 N. Robert
First Floor
St. Paul, MN   55101
612/296-6426

9401 James Avenue S,
Suite 185
Bloomington, MN   55431
612/341-7511

MISSISSIPPI
1520 W. Capitol Street
PO Box 1699
Jackson, MS   38215
601/961-7528

1100 17th Avenue
PO Box 750
Meridian, MS   39302
601/483-1406

MISSOURI
421 E. Dunklin Street
PO Box 59
Jefferson City, MO   65104
314/751-3215

1411 Main Street
Kansas City, MO   64105
816/889-3000

NEVADA
500 E. 3rd Street
Carson City, NV   89713
702/687-4601

70 W. Taylor Street
Reno, NV   89520
702/688-1392

NEW HAMPSHIRE
32 S. Main Street
Concord, NH   03301
603/224-3311

317 Lincoln Street
Manchester, NH   03103
603/627-7841

NEW JERSEY
87 Newkirk Street,
1st Floor
Jersey City, NJ   07306
201/795-8862

28 Yard Avenue, Room 29
Trenton, NJ   08609
609/292-0620

NEW MEXICO
PO Box 1928
Albuquerque, NM 87103
505/841-8457

301 W. Devargas Street
Santa Fe, NM 87501
505/827-3737

OHIO
145 S. Front Street
Columbus, OH 43216
614/644-7096

1810-1814 Madison Avenue
PO Box 954
Toledo, OH 43624
419/245-2956

OKLAHOMA
305 Will Rogers Memorial
State Office Bldg.
Oklahoma City, OK 73105
405/557-7235

3105 E. Skelly Drive
Tulsa, OK 74105
918/749-6864

OREGON
875 Union Street NE
Room 201
Salem, OR 97311
503/378-2049

1433 SW 6th Avenue
PO Box 159
Portland, OR 97207
503/229-5730

PENNSYLVANIA
7th & Forster Streets
Room 1118
Harrisburg, PA 17121
717/787-6338

1316 State Street
Erie, PA 16501
814/871-4229

RHODE ISLAND
101 Friendship Street
Providence, RI 02903
401/277-3722

217/219 Pond Street
PO Box 119
Woonsocket, RI 02895

SOUTH CAROLINA
1550 Gadsden Street
PO Box 1406
Columbia, SC 29202
803/737-2588

176 Lockwood Drive
PO Drawer N
Charleston, SC 29402
803/792-7032

SOUTH DAKOTA
420 S. Roosevelt
PO Box 4730
Aberdeen, SD 57401
605/622-2314

817 W. Russell Street
PO Box 778
Sioux Falls, SD 57101
605/339-6580

TENNESSEE
500 James Robertson Pkwy,
11th Floor
Nashville, TN 37245
615/741-1792

1295 Poplar Avenue
PO Box 40859
Memphis, TN 38174
901/543-7852

TEXAS
101 E. 15th Street, #404 T
Austin, TX 78778
512/463-2623

811 N. Westmorland
Dallas, TX 75211
214/330-0364

UTAH
720 S. 2nd East
Salt Lake City, UT 84147
801/536-7000

PO Box 1339
Provo, UT 84603
801/373-7500

VERMONT
5 Green Mountain Drive
PO Box 488
Montpelier, VT 05602
802/229-0311

232 Main Street
PO Box 814
Brattleboro, VT 05301
802/254-4555

VIRGINIA
703 E. Main St, Room 327
PO Box 1358
Richmond, VA 23211
804/786-8823

5145 E. Virginia Beach Blvd.
Norfolk, VA 23502
804/455-3900

WASHINGTON
605 Woodview Drive
Olympia, WA 98504
206/438-4104

PO Box 91313
Bellevue, WA 98009
206/455-7113

WEST VIRGINIA
112 California Avenue
Charleston, WV 25305
304/348-3452

914 5th Avenue
Box 970
Huntington, WV 25713
304/528-5525

WISCONSIN
206 N. Broom Street
Madison, WI 53703
608/266-1492

330 S. Jefferson Street
Green Bay, WI 54301
414/448-5019

WYOMING
100 W. Midwest Street
PO Box 2760
Casper, WY 82602
307/235-3252

18th & Bent Streets
PO Box 706
Cheyenne, WY 82003
307/777-7811

APPENDIX 6

The following is a partial listing of job descriptions in GS level order.

CORRECTIONAL INSTITUTION ADMINISTRATOR

Correctional Institution Administrators (GS-0007) manage, or participate in the overall management of, correctional institutions, systems, or programs. They also advise, review, and evaluate the management of correctional institutions, systems, or programs. Work in this series requires knowledge of phenological theories, principles, and techniques and the problems, methods, and techniques of institutional management.

SAFETY & OCCUPATIONAL HEALTH MANAGERS

Safety and Occupational Health Managers (GS-0018) manage, administer, or operate safety and occupational health programs, or perform administrative work concerned with safety and occupational health activities, or develop, implement, and evaluate related program functions. Their primary objective is to design effective management policies, programs, or practices which eliminate or minimize: human injury, and property and productivity losses.

SAFETY TECHNICIANS

Safety Technicians (GS-0019) support work in accident prevention. This includes: inspecting safety conditions, investigating and compiling data on accidents, and providing information on safety standards and techniques.

OUTDOOR RECREATION PLANNERS

Outdoor Recreation Planners (GS-0023) plan, advise, and coordinate the use of land, water, and related resources. They provide opportunities for the creative use of leisure time outdoors, while protecting and enhancing the quality of the outdoor environment for the enjoyment of people.

PARK RANGERS

Park Rangers (GS-0025) supervise, manage, and/or perform work in the conservation and use of Federal park resources. This involves: park conservation, natural, historical, and cultural resource management & the development and operation of interpretive and recreational programs for the benefit of the public.

ENVIRONMENTAL PROTECTION SPECIALIST

Environmental Protection Specialists (GS-0028) advise and assist state and local government agencies on their environmental protection plans and programs, compliance with Federal standards, and development and review of grant proposals, develop and analyze data and prepare reports on plans for state environmental protection programs.

UNITED STATES MARSHALS

United States Marshals (GS-0082) perform a wide range of law enforcement duties which include: serving a variety of civil writs and criminal warrants issued by Federal courts, tracing and arresting Federal fugitives, seizing and disposing of property under court orders, safeguarding and transporting prisoners, providing for the physical security of court facilities and personnel, jurors, and key government witnesses, preventing civil disturbances or restoring order in riot and mob violence situations, and performing other special law enforcement duties as directed by a court order or the Department of Justice.

POLICE OFFICERS

Police (GS-0083) perform or supervise work in: the preservation of the peace, the prevention, detection, and investigation of crimes, the arrest or apprehension of violators, and the provision of assistance to citizens in emergency situations, including the protection of civil rights.

NUCLEAR MATERIALS COURIERS

Nuclear Materials Couriers (GS-084) perform or supervise the safe and secure transportation of sensitive nuclear material owned or controlled by the Department of Energy. The work requires knowledge of laws, rules, regulations, methods, techniques, and procedures governing: the operation, control, and protection of vehicles and their cargoes; the use of tactical weapons and arrest authority; emergencies involving health and safety of personnel, vehicles, and nuclear materials; departmental and other Federal, State, and local security authorities; and similar knowledge involving the protection, movement, and delivery of sensitive nuclear materials.

SECURITY CLERICAL AND ASSISTANT

Security and Clerical Assistants (GS-0086) perform clerical and assistant tasks in support of established security programs (e.g., personnel, physical, information, or industrial security) when such work requires, in addition to general administrative and/or clerical skills, practical knowledge of specific security objectives, programs, methods, and procedures, and skills in carrying out support tasks related to security administration.

GUIDES

Guides (GS-0090) provide or supervise nonprofessional interpretive and guide services to visitors to parks, dams and other sites of public interest. The work involves giving formal talks, interpreting natural and historic features, explaining engineering structures and related water resource developments, answering questions, guiding tours, and providing miscellaneous services to visitors. Incidental duties are performed in connection with responsibility for visitor safety and protection of historic and scientific objects and natural or engineering features.

INTELLIGENCE SPECIALISTS

Intelligence Specialists (GS-0132) deal with information that directly or indirectly affects the national security. More specifically, they: advise, administer, supervise, or perform work in the collection, analysis, evaluation, interpretation, and dissemination of information on political, economic, social, cultural, physical, geographic, scientific, or military conditions, trends, and forces in foreign and domestic areas.

GEOGRAPHERS

Geographers (GS-0150) perform professional work in the field of geography. They deal with such natural and human phenomena as: physical features of the earth, climate, plant and animal life, and man's settlements and institutions. Geographers compile, synthesize, analyze, interpret and present information regarding the location, distribution, and interrelationships and processes of change affecting the phenomena mentioned above.

HISTORIANS

Historians (GS-0170) advise, administer, supervise or perform research or other work in the field of history. The duties include collecting, evaluating, analyzing, or presenting historical facts. The position requires professional knowledge of the established methods and techniques of historical research.

PSYCHOLOGY AIDS & TECHNICIANS

Psychology Aids and Technicians (GS-0181) perform nonprofessional technical work in programs of research or direct services. Positions in this series involve a practical understanding of some of the principles, methods and techniques of psychology, but do not require formal education in psychology.

SOCIAL SERVICE AIDS & ASSISTANTS

Social Service Aids and Assistants (GS-0186) provide support for counseling, guidance, and related social services work. Their clients are individuals or families in the community, or individuals in an institution, dormitory, or other Government facility. Duties may range from: providing group leadership & practical guidance to residents of a Government facility, to giving unemployed adults information and assistance on community job training or employment opportunities. The work requires: effective communication, ability to work constructively with groups, a practical knowledge of program requirements and procedures, and a practical understanding of some of the more routine methods and techniques of counseling.

PERSONNEL CLERKS & ASSISTANTS

Personnel Clerks and Assistants (GS-0203) supervise, lead, or perform: CLERICAL WORK which requires substantial knowledge of personnel terminology, requirements, procedures, and functions. This may involve: processing documents, preparing standard personnel reports, explaining personnel procedures, maintaining master personnel & organizational records, & providing miscellaneous clerical support in personnel related units; LIMITED TECHNICAL WORK which requires substantial practical knowledge of one or more personnel management specialty, such as staffing, employee relations, and classification. This position is different from a personnel management specialist. Clerks and assistants don't need to have as much knowledge or expertise in the Federal personnel system or an in-depth knowledge of personnel management concepts, principles, and techniques.

PERSONNEL STAFFING SPECIALISTS

Personnel Staffing Specialists (GS-0212) perform technical personnel work. They: recruit, examine, select, or place and utilize employees to staff organizations. They need to be able to apply the principles, practices, and techniques of recruitment, examination, selection, and/or placement.

EMPLOYEE RELATIONS SPECIALISTS

Employee Relations Specialists (GS-0230) administer, supervise, evaluate, or perform technical work. They establish and maintain employer-employee relationships that contribute to satisfactory productivity, motivation, morale, and discipline. This involves: providing guidance, consultation, and assistance to management and employees on employee relations matters, & advising on grievances and appeals, adverse actions, employee discipline and related matters.

APPRENTICESHIP & TRAINING REPS

Apprenticeship and Training Specialists (GS-243) administer, supervise, or perform work to: promote apprenticeship and other on-the-job training programs and standards to meet the needs for skilled manpower in industry, and provide technical advice and assistance to improve and obtain more effective use of worker skills on the job, & review standards & training agreements to ensure conformance with national standards.

MESSENGERS

Messengers (GS-302) receive, deliver, and collect incoming and outgoing mail or other documents or items, including correspondence, memoranda, publications, records, files, packages, and other similar material. Some positions may also involve the performance of light manual or mechanical work, or general office tasks of a simple and routine nature, or the operation of a motor vehicle.

MISCELLANEOUS CLERKS & ASSISTANTS

Miscellaneous Clerk and Assistants (GS-303) perform or supervise clerical, assistant, or technical work of a general nature. The work: requires knowledge of the procedures and techniques involved in carrying out the work of an organization, and involves applying procedures and practices within the framework of established guidelines.

MAIL AND FILE CLERKS

Mail and File Clerks (GS-305) administer, supervise, or perform clerical work related to the: processing of incoming or outgoing mail, systematic arrangement of records for storage or reference purposes, and scheduled disposition of records. They may also perform related work that requires: the application of established mail or file methods and procedures, knowledge of prescribed systems for governing the flow and control of communications, filing or storage and retrieval of records, and knowledge of the organization and functions of the operating unit or units serviced.

SECRETARIES

Secretaries (GS-318) assist one individual, and in some cases the subordinate staff of that individual. This involves performing general office work that is auxiliary to the work of the organization. A secretary is the principal office clerk or administrative support person in the office. The work requires: a knowledge of clerical and administrative procedures and requirements, various office skills, and the ability to teach such skills in a way that increases the effectiveness of others. The duties do not require a technical or professional knowledge of a specialized subject matter area.

CLERK TYPISTS

Clerk-Typists (GS-322) produce typed documents from written material or voice recordings. They may also do general clerical work, but typing is their main function. Clerk typists may also supervise other clerk typists.

COMPUTER OPERATORS

Computer Operators (GS-332) operate or supervise the operation of the controls of a digital computer system. They may also operate peripheral equipment if the equipment is directly related to the system or its use. Operators must: know the functions of the various computer features, and have the skill to read, interpret, and correctly respond to information in the form in which it is transmitted through the computer system.

PROGRAM MANAGERS

Program Managers (GS-340) manage or direct one or more programs, including appropriate supporting service organizations. The paramount qualification requirement of the positions is management and executive knowledge and ability. The positions do not require competence in a specialized subject-matter or functional area. (Positions in which specialized subject matter or functional competence is a necessary qualification requirement are classifiable in whichever specialized or general series is most appropriate.)

ADMINISTRATIVE OFFICERS

Administrative Officers (GS-341) provide or obtain a variety of management services that are essential to the direction and operation of an organization. The work requires: extensive knowledge and understanding of management principles, practices, methods and techniques, and skill in integrating management services with the general management of an organization.

PRINTING CLERKS

Printing Clerks (GS-351) need to have knowledge of clerical procedures and operations peculiar to the control, procurement, or providing of printing services. For instance, they process requisitions for procurement of printing, identify from agency guides established specifications, estimate costs for standard recurring publications, maintain control records for production or cost purposes, etc. A technical knowledge of printing as required for Printing Managers is not required for performance of work in this occupation.

EQUAL OPPORTUNITY ASSISTANTS

Equal Opportunity Assistants (GS-361) supervise or perform technical and substantive clerical work in support of equal opportunity and civil rights programs or activities. The paramount qualification requirement is a practical knowledge of the methods, procedures, regulations, and purposes of the equal opportunity or civil rights function the positions support. This occupation does not require the broad knowledge of equal opportunity and civil rights principles, or the depth of skill in analysis, interpretation, and decision-making characteristic of Equal Opportunity Compliance Specialists, Equal Employment Opportunity Specialists, and Civil Rights Analysts.

TOXICOLOGISTS

Toxicologists (GS-415) administer, advise on, supervise, or perform research, analytical, advisory, or other professional and scientific work in the discipline of toxicology. They study the adverse effects of chemical substances or similar agents on living organisms and/or environment, and the assessment of the probability of their occurrence under specified conditions of use or exposure. Toxicology:

(1)   involves the study of the interaction of chemical and physical agents and biological systems, the exploration of the nature and mechanisms of adverse reactions, and the assessment of the likelihood that adverse effects will occur; and

(2)   requires the application of scientific knowledge including, but not limited to, pathology, anatomy, chemistry, biochemistry, microbiology, physiology, pharmacology, toxicology, and materials sciences (e.g., as they pertain to the interrelationships of composition, structure, and properties), but does not require full preparation for practice in any one of those disciplines, or full professional training in medicine or veterinary science.

WILDLIFE BIOLOGISTS

Wildlife Biologists (GS-486) perform professional and scientific biological work, rather than managing wildlife refuges. They: conserve and manage wildlife resources, or determine, establish, and apply the biological facts, principles, methods, techniques, and procedures necessary to conserve and manage wildlife resources.

ACCOUNTANTS

Accountants (GS-510) advise, administer, supervise, or perform professional accounting work related to the transactions of government, quasi-government, or private business organizations. They: design, develop, install, operate, or inspect accounting systems, prescribe accounting requirements, audit or examine accounts and records of transactions, examine, analyze, and interpret accounting data or reports, or provide accounting advice and assistance to management.

AUDITORS

Auditors (GS-511) systematically examine and appraise: financial records, financial and management reports, and management controls, policies and practices which affect or reflect the financial condition and operating results of an activity. They also perform analytical work to develop and execute audit policies and programs. This work requires the application of professional accounting knowledge, standards, and principles.

BUDGET CLERKS & ASSISTANTS

Budget Clerks and Assistants (GS-561) perform clerical and technical work in support of budget analysis and administration. The work requires: knowing the procedures which facilitate budgeting as it is conducted in the Federal service, a practical understanding of, and skill in applying the administrative rules, regulations, and procedures associated with: recording, reporting, processing, and keeping track of budgetary transactions.

TAX EXAMINERS

Tax Examiners (GS-592) perform or supervise work in the Internal Revenue Service. They may: process original tax returns, establish tax account records or change such records based on later information affecting taxes and refunds, collect taxes and/or obtain tax returns, compute or verify tax, penalty and interest, and determine proper tax liability.

PHYSICIAN'S ASSISTANTS

Physician's Assistants (GS-603) provide diagnostic and therapeutic medical care and services under the guidance of the physician. They do not interpret medical findings that require a physician's license. Physician's assistants examine and observe patients by: taking case histories, conducting physical examinations, and ordering laboratory studies during hospital rounds and visits to clinics. While under the guidance of a physician, they carry out special procedures such as: giving injections or other medication, applying or changing dressing, performing lumbar punctures, or suturing minor lacerations.

MEDICAL SUPPLY AIDS & TECHNICIANS

Medical Supply Aides and Technicians (GS-622) provide wards, clinics, operating rooms, and other hospital facilities with medical supplies, instruments, sets, and equipment. The work requires knowing: aseptic techniques and sterilization practices, the care, functioning, and uses of supplies, equipment, sets, and instruments, methods for preparing, storing, and issuing sterile and non-sterile medical supplies, and how to maintain adequate stock levels.

MEDICAL MACHINE TECHNICIANS

Medical Machine Technicians (GS-649) perform nonprofessional technical work, which is subordinate to the work of physicians or other professional or scientific employees. The work includes monitoring: medical machines, equipment (except radiographic medical equipment), or instruments as part of the examination or treatment of human patients. The work requires a knowledge of: the techniques of operating and day-to-day maintenance of one or more kinds of nonradiographic medical machines, equipment, or instruments, and human anatomy and physiology, and possibly chemistry and/or mathematics.

PHARMACISTS

Pharmacists (GS-660) perform professional and scientific work in the field of pharmacy. The work typically involves: compounding prescriptions of physicians, dentists, and other licensed practitioners, formulating, preparing, bulk compounding, selecting, dispensing and preserving drugs, medicines, and chemicals, researching the development of special vehicles or variations of standard formulas to meet the needs of individual patients,developing original techniques of compounding and making available for use new investigational drugs, advising on drug therapy and usage, or performing administrative or advisory work to administer a pharmacy program for a hospital, clinic, or other medical care facility, and possibly evaluating drug proposals submitted by private industry, and monitoring marketed drugs for safety and efficency.

ORTHOTISTS & PROSTHETISTS

Orthotists and Prosthetists (GS-667) design, fabricate, or fit orthotic or prosthetic devices. This is done to preserve or restore function to patients with disabling conditions of the limbs and spine or with partial or total absence of limbs. The work requires: knowledge of anatomy, physiology, body mechanics, the application and function of orthoses (braces and orthopedic shoes) and prostheses (artificial

143

limbs), and of the materials available for the fabrication of such devices, skill in the use of tools and specialized equipment, and the ability to deal effectively with patients and their problems and to work with other members of the medical team.

MEDICAL RECORD LIBRARIANS

Medical Record Librarians (GS-669) advise, supervise or perform work which involves applying the accepted theories and techniques of medical record library science. They develop, maintain, analyze, and use diagnostic and therapeutic medical records. All positions in this category include one or more of the following technical functions: advising management or staff members, or providing consultation services, on medical record problems and procedures, advising research investigators or staff members on methods of recording or retrieving record data, teaching or training personnel or staff members in medical record techniques or closely related subjects, evaluating and modifying a medical record program to meet particular needs, organizing or managing a medical record program, or advising on or being responsible for medical record matters involving medico-legal problems.

HEALTH SYSTEM ADMINISTRATORS

Health System Administrators (GS-670) apply the specialized principles and practices of health care management. They have full line responsibility for the administrative management of a health care delivery system. The systems may range from a nationwide network including many hospitals to a major subdivision of an individual hospital. The fundamental responsibility of a health system administrator is to effectively use all available resources to provide the best possible patient care. Meeting this responsibility requires: an understanding of the critical balance between the administrative and clinical functions in the health care delivery system, and the ability to coordinate and control programs and resources to achieve this balance. A physician's license is not necessary to qualify for this position.

HEALTH SYSTEM SPECIALISTS

Health System Specialists (GS-671) support health care management officials by analyzing, evaluating, advising, and/or coordinating health care delivery systems and operations. They do not have the full line responsibility that Health System Administrators possess. The position may be located within an operating health care facility or at a higher organizational level. The work requires: a high degree of analytical ability, specialized knowledge of the basic principles and practices related to the management of health care delivery systems.

HOSPITAL HOUSEKEEPERS

Hospital Housekeeping Managers (GS-673) need administrative ability and technical knowledge to supervise or perform work in developing, coordinating, directing, and managing hospital housekeeping programs. The major concern of such programs is sanitation. The hospital must not only look clean, but also be free of bacteria and other health hazards.

MEDICAL RECORD TECHNICIANS

Medical Record Technicians (GS-675) analyze medical records for completeness, consistency, and compliance with requirements, and perform related functions such as: coding medical record information, and selecting and compiling medical record data. The work requires applying a practical knowledge of: medical terminology, anatomy, physiology, the internal organization and consistency of the medical record, medical record references and procedures, and the medical and legal significance of medical records.

MEDICAL CLERKS

Medical Clerks (GS-679) perform clerical work to support the care and treatment given to patients in a ward, clinic or other unit of a medical facility. This work includes functions such as: serving as a receptionist, performing record keeping duties, performing clerical duties relating to patient care and treatment, and providing miscellaneous support to the medical staff of the unit. The work requires a practical knowledge of: the medical facility's organization and services, the basic rules and regulations governing visitors and patient treatment, and the standard procedures, medical records and medical terminology of the unit supported.

INDUSTRIAL HYGIENISTS

Industrial Hygienists (GS-690) perform professional and scientific work in industrial hygiene. This includes: identifying and evaluating conditions affecting the health and efficiency of employees, or the citizens of the adjacent community, formulating and recommending measures to eliminate or control occupational health hazards, and promoting occupational health programs for instructing and motivating managers and employees in the prevention and correction of potential health hazards.

CONSUMER SAFETY OFFICERS

Consumer Safety Specialists (GS-696) enforce the laws and regulations that protect consumers from foods, drugs, cosmetics, fabrics, toys, and household products and equipment that are: impure, unwholesome, ineffective, improperly or deceptively labeled or packaged, or in some other way dangerous or defective. These positions require knowledge of various scientific fields such as chemistry, biology, pharmacology, and food technology. Consumer safety officers: identify substances and sources of adulteration and contamination, and evaluate manufacturing practices, production processes, quality control systems, laboratory analyses, and clinical investigation programs.

SAFETY ENGINEERS

Safety Engineers (GS-803) perform professional engineering work to eliminate or control hazardous conditions which may lead to personal injury or damaged property. The hazardous conditions are often the result of human error, or equipment and machine malfunctions. The work requires applying: advanced mathematical techniques, professional engineering principles, methods, and techniques, safety related elements of the physical sciences, ergonomics, psychology and physiology, and safety principles, standards, practices, and analytical techniques.

FIRE PREVENTION ENGINEERS

Fire Prevention Engineers (GS-804) advise, administer, supervise, or perform research or other professional and scientific work. They may: investigate or develop fire prevention projects, design, construct, inspect, test, operate, or maintain fire fighting or fire prevention apparatus and systems, or test fire resistent materials.

MATERIALS ENGINEERS

Materials Engineers (GS-806) perform professional work of a general nature in engineering or physical sciences. Their primary concerns are the properties, processing, uses, and inservice behavior of engineering materials. The work requires: a highly developed knowledge of materials and their properties, processing, uses, and behavior under environmental influences, an understanding of and the ability to utilize advances of the fundamental materials sciences, e.g., as they pertain to the interrelationships of composition, structure, and properties, and knowledge of and ability to apply pertinent engineering principles and practices including considerations such as cost, availability, fabrication, performance, and use.

CIVIL ENGINEERS

Civil Engineers (GS-810) manage, supervise, or perform professional work in the field of civil engineering. Typically, they must: be able to apply a general knowledge of the physical sciences and mathematics which underlie engineering, and possess a specialized knowledge of mechanics of solids, particularly soils, hydraulics, theory of structure, strength of materials, engineering geology, and surveying. The work involves: planning, designing, constructing, and/or maintaining structures and facilities that provide shelter, support transportation systems, and control natural resources, investigating, measuring, surveying and mapping the earth's physical features and phenomena, and research and development activities.

SURVEYING TECHNICIANS

Surveying Technicians (GS-817) apply the technical knowledge of surveying methods, equipment, and techniques. They measure or determine distances, elevations, areas, angles, land boundaries, and other features of the earth's surface. Surveying specializations specifically included in this category are: topographic, hydrographic, geodetic, land, control, and construction surveying.

COMPUTER ENGINEERS

Computer Engineers (GS-854) apply knowledge in the following areas:

(a)   fundamentals and principles of professional engineering,
(b)   computer hardware, systems software, and computer system architecture and integration, and
(c)   mathematics, including calculus, probability, statistics discrete structures, and modern algebra.

The work pertains primarily to the research, design, development, testing, evaluation, and maintenance of computer hardware and software systems in an integrated manner.

ELECTRONICS ENGINEERS

Electronics Engineers (GS-855) perform professional work that requires applying knowledge of: physical and engineering sciences and mathematics, electronic phenomena, and the principles, techniques, and practices of electronics engineering. The work pertains primarily to: electronic circuits, circuit elements, and electro-magnetic or acoustical wave energy or electrical information as they are used to: communicate, compute, sense, control, measure, and navigate.

ELECTRONICS TECHNICIANS

Electronics Technicians (GS-856) perform work that requires knowledge of electronics engineering, but not to the extent required for a professional position. The requirements include: knowledge of the techniques and theories characteristic of electronics such as a basic knowledge of electricity and electronic theory, algebra, and elementary physics.

AEROSPACE ENGINEERS

Aerospace Engineers (GS-861) perform work which involves: planning, researching, developing, designing, testing, evaluating, producing, fabricating, operating, and maintaining aerospace vehicles and integrally associated equipment, and investigating phenomena encountered in aerospace flight.

AGRICULTURAL ENGINEERS

Agricultural Engineers (GS-890) perform professional work which requires knowledge of the principles of engineering and agriculture in order to solve agricultural problems. Agricultural problems which may be solved by an agricultural engineer include such areas as: farm structures, soil and water conservation, mechanical power and machinery, and electric power and processing.

CHEMICAL ENGINEERS

Chemical Engineers (GS-893) perform professional work which involves changes in the chemical composition or physical state of materials. It requires applying the principles and practices of chemical engineering, chemistry, and other scientific and engineering disciplines. The work may involve a wide range of duties including: researching, developing, designing, operating, evaluating, and improving processes, plants, equipment, methods, or products.

INDUSTRIAL ENGINEERING TECHNICIANS

Industrial Engineering Technicians (GS-895) perform nonprofessional technical work. They plan, design, analyze, and install work systems which integrate men, materials, and equipment in order to: produce products, render services, repair equipment, or move and store supplies and equipment.

ADMINISTRATIVE LAW JUDGES

Administrative Law Judges (GS-935) perform professional work that involves conducting formal hearings. These hearings are required by statute, in accordance with the Administrative Procedure Act (Public Law 79-404).

PARALEGAL SPECIALISTS

Paralegal Specialists (GS-950) perform work that does not require graduation from a recognized law school. Training may be gained from a professional or educational institution, or supervised on-the-job assignments. The work requires discretion and independent judgment to apply specialized knowledge of the laws, precedent decisions, regulations, agency policies and practices, and judicial or administrative proceedings. Some positions also require a practical knowledge of the agency's substantive programs. The specialists may: analyze the legal impact of legislative developments and administrative and judicial decisions, conduct research for the preparation of legal opinions on matters of interest to the agency, and perform substantive legal analysis of requests for information under the provisions of various acts.

VISA & PASSPORT EXAMINERS

Visa and Passport Examiners (GS-967) administer, advise, supervise, or perform quasi-legal work. They review, evaluate and examine applications for: United States passports, and other privileges and services that involve citizenship determinations, and/or United States visas, and other privileges and services that involve determinations of eligibility for admission to this country.

LEGAL CLERKS & TECHNICIANS

Legal Clerks and Technicians (GS-986) perform or supervise clerical or technical work of a general nature. The work requires: a specialized knowledge of legal documents & processes, & the ability to apply established instructions, rules, regulations, precedents, and procedures pertaining to legal activities.

UNEMPLOYMENT COMP CLAIM EXAMINERS

Unemployment Compensation Claims Examiners (GS-994) administer, supervise, or perform quasi-legal work. They develop, examine, adjust, reconsider, or authorize the settlement of claims for unemployment compensation, including sickness benefits.

VETERANS CLAIMS EXAMINERS

Veterans Claims Examiners (GS-996) administer, supervise, or perform quasi-legal work. They develop, examine, adjust, reconsider, or authorize the settlement of claims filed by veterans or their dependents and beneficiaries. These claims may be in regard to: disability compensation, disability, pension, death pension, death compensation, National Service Life Insurance, and U.S. Government Life Insurance, and other benefits administered by the Department of Veterans' Affairs.

CIVIL SERVICE RETIREMENT CLAIMS EXAMINER

Civil Service Retirement Claims Examiners (GS-997) perform quasi-legal work. They examine, develop, and adjudicate claims for benefits under the amended Civil Service Retirement Act. The work requires a knowledge of the laws and regulations which relate to this retirement and insurance program.

CLAIMS CLERKS

Claims Clerks (GS-998) perform clerical work. They examine, review, or develop claims by or against the Federal Government. The clerical positions included in this category are those concerned with: examining and developing claims cases for adjudication, determining and verifying entitlement to benefits, where the legal requirements are clear and the examination process is routine.

PHOTOGRAPHERS

Photographers (GS-1060) perform: still, motion picture, television, high-speed, aerial, or other similar camera work, or photographic processing work, or a combination of these two types of work. In addition to knowledge of the equipment, techniques, and processes of photography, the work requires either: knowledge of the work to be photographed in such fields as science, engineering, technical and medical research and operations, or artistic ability in: selecting, arranging, and lighting subjects, or processing negatives, or printing, enlarging, cropping, or retouching prints.

WRITERS AND EDITORS

Writers and Editors (GS-1082) write, rewrite, or edit: reports, articles, news stories and releases, which are to appear in publications, reports, periodicals, or the press, or speeches that are to be presented in person, or by means of radio or television, or radio, television, or motion picture scripts. The work requires the ability to: acquire information about different subjects, and analyze, select, and present the information in a form suitable for the intended audience. It does not require substantial subject-matter knowledge.

TECHNICAL WRITERS & EDITORS

Technical Writers and Editors (GS-1083) perform or supervise writing and/or editing. The work requires applying: substantial subject-matter knowledge, and writing and editing skills, including the ability to determine the type of presentation best suited to the audience. This category does not include work which requires substantial, but not full professional or technical subject-matter knowledge.

CONTRACT SPECIALISTS

Contract Specialists (GS-1102) manage, supervise, & develop policies & procedures, or perform work involving the: procurement of supplies, services, construction, or research and development by using formal advertising or negotiation procedures, evaluation of contract price proposals, and the administration or termination of contracts.

PROPERTY DISPOSAL SPECIALISTS

Property Disposal Specialists (GS-1104) perform administrative, managerial, or technical work concerned with the utilization, redistribution, donation, sale, or other disposition of excess or surplus personal property in Government activities.

PROCUREMENT CLERKS & ASSISTANTS

Procurement Clerks and Assistants (GS-1106) perform clerical and technical support work that involves: purchases, procurement, and contract negotiation, administration, and termination. Typical work includes: preparing, controlling, verifying, or abstracting procurement documents, reports, or industry publications or other clerical and support work related to procurement operations, and technical work in support of such contract and procurement tasks.

COMMISSARY STORE MANAGERS

Commissary Store Managers (GS-1144) manage, supervise, or advise on the operation of: commissary stores, the departments of commissary stores, or overall commissary operations. The work requires knowledge of: commercial retail food merchandising, and food store management.

INTERNAL REVENUE OFFICERS

Internal Revenue Officers (GS-1169) perform work that involves: collecting delinquent taxes, canvassing for unreported taxes due, and securing delinquent returns. The work requires knowledge of; general or specialized business practices, internal revenue laws, regulations, procedures and precedents, judicial processes, laws of evidence, and the interrelationship between Federal and State laws with respect to the collection and assessment processes, and investigative techniques and methods.

APPRAISERS AND ASSESSORS

Appraisers and Assessors (GS-1171) supervise or perform work to appraise real or personal property or the interests therein. The position requires technical knowledge and skill in the application of the principles, practices, and techniques of appraisal.

BUILDING MANAGERS

Building Managers (GS-1176) manage public buildings or other facilities. They provide occupant organizations with appropriate space and essential building services in order to promote occupant welfare, safety, and productivity. Positions in this series typically involve one or more of the following functions: directly managing, or assisting in managing, the operation of one or more public buildings and surrounding grounds, directing comprehensive building management programs, or performing staff level work in the study of building management methods and the development of standard building management practices. The work requires: management and administrative skills, the ability to meet and deal effectively with a wide variety of individuals and groups, and knowledge of building operational requirements.

HEALTH PHYSICISTS

Health Physicists (GS-1306) protect man and his environment from unwarranted exposure to ionizing radiation. The work requires professional knowledge and competence in health physics.

HYDROLOGY TECHNICIANS

Hydrologic Technicians (GS-1316) work as aids and technicians in a field of science concerned with the study of water, its quantity, quality, availability, movement, and distribution. The work includes: applying practical knowledge of: hydrologic methods and techniques, and the construction, application, operation, and limitations of instruments, equipment, and materials used in hydrologic investigations.

OCEANOGRAPHERS

Oceanographers (GS-1360) perform professional, scientific work which requires a fundamental background in chemistry, physics and mathematics and appropriate knowledge in the field of oceanography. They: collect, measure, analyze, evaluate and interpret natural and physical ocean phenomena, such as currents, physical and submarine features, depth, organic and inorganic sediments, and heat exchange, and their interrelations with other marine phenomena (e.g., weather, geological structure, etc.), and plan, organize, conduct, and administer seagoing and land-based study and research of ocean phenomena for the purpose of interpreting, predicting, utilizing and controlling ocean forces and events.

NAVIGATIONAL INFO SPECIALISTS

Navigational Information Specialists (GS-1361) perform work involving the: acquisition, collection, evaluation, selection, and preparation of vital aeronautical or marine information. They disseminate the information in official publications concerning safe navigation and related operations.

LAND SURVEYORS

Land Surveyors (GS-1373) perform professional work in land surveying. They: establish, investigate, and reestablish land and property boundaries, and prepare plats and legal descriptions for tracts of land. The work requires knowledge of: the concepts, principles and techniques of surveying, including underlying mathematics and physical science, & land ownership laws.

FOOD TECHNOLOGISTS

Food Technologists (GS-1382) perform professional work to study and analyze problems related to: developing, improving, and evaluating food products, utilizing, processing and preserving them, and utilizing or disposing of by-products.

LIBRARIANS

Librarians (GS-1410) perform work that requires: full professional knowledge of the theories, objectives, principles, and techniques of librarianship, a knowledge of literature resources, substantial knowledge of the subject matter involved, and/or substantial knowledge of foreign languages. The work involves: collecting, organizing, preserving, and retrieving recorded knowledge in printed, written, audiovisual, film, wax, near-print methods, magnetic tape, or other media, selecting, acquiring, cataloging, and classifying: materials, bibliographic and readers' advisory services, reference and literature searching services, library management and systems planning, or developing and strengthening library services.

COMPUTER SCIENCE SPECIALISTS

Computer Science Specialists (GS-1550) apply or research computer science methods and techniques to store, manipulate, transform or present information by means of computer systems. The work requires: applying the theoretical foundations of computer science, including computer system architecture and system software organization, the representation and transformation of information structure, and the theoretical models involved.

GENERAL FACILITIES & EQUIPMENT MANAGER

Facilities and Equipment Specialists (GS-1601) perform work that: combines the characteristics of two or more positions that involve facilities and equipment management, or involves equipment, facilities, or services work of such a general or specialized nature that it is not included in any other categories.

CEMETERY ADMINISTRATORS

Cemetery Superintendents (GS-1630) manage the operation of cemeteries. The work requires the ability to: meet and deal with a variety of people and their problems, plan, budget, schedule, coordinate, and supervise cemetery activities, and apply knowledge of applicable regulations, techniques, and operating practices.

PRINTING SPECIALISTS

Printing Specialists (GS-1654) plan, administer, supervise, review, evaluate, or perform work in order to manage programs which provide printing services. They may also supervise related functions such as editing, illustrating, and distributing printed materials.

LAUNDRY/DRY CLEAN PLANT MANAGER

Laundry and Dry Cleaning Plant Managers (GS-1658) advise, manage and direct the operation of a laundry, a dry cleaning plant, or a combined laundry and dry cleaning plant. The work requires: skill in performing managerial functions associated with the operation of a laundry and/or dry cleaning plants, & a combination of a practical knowledge of laundry and/or dry cleaning equipment and processing operations.

STEWARDS

Stewards (GS-1667) manage, supervise, or perform work involved in the operation of the food supply service of a Government institution, including a storeroom, kitchen, dining room, meat shop, and bakery.

EQUIPMENT SPECIALISTS

Equipment Specialists (GS-1670) supervise or perform work to: collect, analyze, interpret, and develop specialized information about equipment, provide such information together with advisory service to those who design, test, produce, procure, supply, operate, repair, or dispose of equipment, and/or develop, install, inspect, or revise equipment maintenance programs and techniques based on a practical knowledge of the equipment, including its design, production, operation and maintenance requirements. Such duties require applying an intensive, practical knowledge of the characteristics, properties, and uses of equipment. This knowledge is gained from technical training, education and experience in such functions as repairing, overhauling, maintaining, constructing, or inspecting equipment.

EDUCATION & TRAINING SPECIALIST

Education and Training Specialists (GS-1701) perform research or other professional work in the field of education and training. The work is of such a general or specialized nature that the positions are not included in any other job categories.

EDUCATION & TRAINING TECHNICIAN

Education and Training Technicians (GS-1702) perform nonprofessional work of a technical, specialized, or support nature in the field of education and training. The work requires: knowledge of the program objectives, policies, procedures, or pertinent regulatory requirements affecting the particular education or training activity, the ability to apply specialized skills and a practical understanding of the particular education or training activities involved.

EDUCATIONAL & VOCATIONAL TRAINING SPECIALIST

Education and Vocational Training Specialists (GS-1710) apply full professional knowledge of the theories, principles, and techniques of education and training in such areas as: instruction, guidance counseling, education administration, development or evaluation of curricula, instructional materials and aids, and educational tests and measurements.

TRAINING INSTRUCTORS

Training Instructors (GS-1712) perform work as an instructor. They may: develop, administer, supervise, and evaluate, training programs. The work requires a combination of practical knowledge of: the methods and techniques of instruction, and the subject matter being taught. Professional knowledge and training in the field of education, or mastery of a trade, craft, or occupation are not the primary requirements for the position.

VOCATIONAL REHABILITATION SPECIALIST

Vocational Rehabilitation Specialists (GS-1715) deal with the vocational rehabilitation problems of the physically or mentally disabled, or of other individuals whose backgrounds and lack of job skills impairs their employability. The work involves: counseling these individuals, planning training programs for them, placing them in gainful employment, and supervising them while in training and during their adjustment to the job.

EDUCATIONAL PROGRAM SPECIALIST

Educational Program Specialists (GS-1720) promote, coordinate, and improve education policies, programs, standards, activities, and opportunities in accordance with national policies and objectives.

PUBLIC HEALTH EDUCATORS

Public Health Educators (GS-1725) administer, supervise, or perform research or other professional work in public health education. They provide leadership, advice, staff assistance, and consultation on health education programs.

INSPECTORS, INVESTIGATORS & COMPLIANCE SPECIALISTS

General Inspectors, Investigators, and Compliance Specialists (GS-1801) assure that others understand and comply with Federal laws, regulations, and other mandatory guidelines. They administer, coordinate, supervise or perform inspections, investigative, analytical, or advisory work. Their work is of such a general or specific nature that it is not included in any other category.

COMPLIANCE INSPECTORS & SUPPORT SPECIALISTS

Compliance Inspectors and Support Specialists (GS-1802) perform or supervise support work of a technical nature. They assure compliance with or enforcement of Federal laws, regulations, or other mandatory guidelines.

GENERAL INVESTIGATORS

General Investigators (GS-1810) plan and conduct investigations dealing with the character, practices, suitability, or qualifications of people or organizations seeking, claiming, or receiving Federal benefits, permits, or employment. The results of these investigation are used to make or invoke administrative judgments, sanctions, or penalties.

CRIMINAL INVESTIGATORS

Criminal Investigators (GS-1811) plan and conduct investigations which relate to alleged or suspected violations of criminal laws.

GAME LAW ENFORCEMENT AGENTS

Game Law Enforcement Agents (GS-1812) administer, coordinate, supervise, or perform inspections, investigative, or advisory work to: assure public understanding of and compliance with Federal statutes and regulations for the conservation of fish and wildlife resources, obtain information on the general condition of such resources, and conduct operations to abate damage to agricultural crops caused by unusual concentrations of wildlife.

AIR SAFETY INVESTIGATORS

Air Safety Investigators (GS-1815) investigate and prevent accidents and incidents involving United States aircraft anywhere in the world. They also establish programs and procedures to notify and report accidents.

IMMIGRATION INSPECTORS

Immigration Inspectors (GS-1816) perform inspection or examining work. They enforce and administer laws which relate to the right of persons to enter, reside in, or depart from the United States, Puerto Rico, Guam, and the Virgin Islands.

MINE SAFETY & HEALTH INSPECTOR

Mine Safety and Health Inspectors (GS-1822) perform or supervise work to: enforce, develop, advise, or interpret mine safety and health laws, regulations, standards, and practices.

AVIATION SAFETY INSPECTORS

Aviation Safety Inspectors (GS-1825) develop, administer, or enforce regulations and standards concerning civil aviation safety, including: the airworthiness of aircraft and aircraft systems, the competence of pilots, mechanics, and other airmen, & safety aspects of aviation facilities, equipment, and procedures.

SECURITIES COMPLIANCE EXAMINER

Securities Compliance Examiners (GS-1831) determine compliance with the statutory and regulatory requirements of securities acts. They direct, supervise, advise,or perform examinations of registered broker-dealers, investment advisers, and investment companies.

AGRICULTURE COMMODITY WAREHOUSE EXAM

Agricultural Commodity Warehouse Examiners (GS-1850) administer, supervise, or perform work involved in examining storage facilities for agricultural commodities which are: licensed or are to be licensed under Federal law, or approved, or to be approved, under Government contract or agreement.

ALCOHOL, TOBACCO, & FIREARMS INSPECTORS

Alcohol, Tobacco and Firearms Inspectors (GS-1854): qualify and inspect establishments engaged in producing or using alcohol or tobacco products, assure full collection of revenue on alcohol and tobacco products, develop and interpret regulations which apply to these establishments, and develop, analyze, and improve programs, procedures, and techniques to regulate establishments involved in producing and using alcohol and tobacco products.

CONSUMER SAFETY INSPECTORS

Consumer Safety Inspectors (GS-1862) develop and conduct: inspections, investigations, and related sampling and data collection activities in support of the laws and regulations protecting consumers from impure, unsanitary, unwholesome, ineffective, improperly labeled, or dangerous foods, drugs, therapeutic devices, cosmetics, fabrics, toys, and household products.

FOOD INSPECTORS

Food Inspectors (GS-1863) assure that products distributed to the consumer are wholesome, not adulterated, and properly marked, labeled and packaged. They inspect the slaughter, processing, packaging, shipping, and storing of: meat and meat products, poultry and poultry products, fish and fish products, and meat products derived from equines. They also inspect food establishments engaged in these activities in order to determine compliance with law and regulations.

IMPORT SPECIALISTS

Import Specialists (GS-1889) deal with the formal entry of imported merchandise. This involves supervising or performing the work of acceptance, tariff classification, appraisement, allowance of drawback claims, and, in some circumstances, liquidation of merchandise. The major objectives of the work are to: assess customs duties and associated taxes to be paid on imported merchandise, and assure compliance with related laws and regulations.

CUSTOMS INSPECTORS

Customs Inspectors (GS-1890) perform inspections work in the enforcement and administration of laws which govern importing or exporting merchandise. The work requires: knowledge of laws, regulations, policies, and procedures concerning the entry, examination, classification, and release of merchandise.

CUSTOMS ENTRY & LIQUIDATION SPECIALISTS

Customs Entry and Liquidation Specialists (GS-1894) administer, supervise, or perform the work of: examining, accepting, processing, or issuing documents required for the entry of imported merchandise into the United States, initially classifying merchandise covered by the entries, determining customs duties and applicable internal revenue taxes accruing on such merchandise, ascertaining the drawback to be paid on exported articles manufactured with the use of duty-paid or tax-paid imported merchandise or substituted domestic merchandise, determining the validity of protests against liquidation decisions on formal entries.

BORDER PATROL AGENTS

Border Patrol Agents (GS-1896) perform enforcement work concerned with: detecting and preventing the smuggling or illegal entry of aliens into the United States, detecting and apprehending: aliens in violation of the conditions under which they were admitted, aliens at interior points in the United States who entered illegally, aliens falsely claiming United States citizenship or legal status, and producers, vendors and users of counterfeit, altered and genuine documents that are used to circumvent the immigration & nationality laws of the United States, & enforcing criminal provisions of the immigration and nationality laws and regulations of the United States.

CUSTOMS AIDS

Customs Aids (GS-1897) supervise or perform nonprofessional work which involves: clerical duties which require the application of specialized knowledge of pertinent provisions of: the Tariff Act, the Navigation Laws, or other similar customs laws, or quasi-technical duties requiring some, but less than full, technical training.

QUALITY ASSURANCE SPECIALISTS

Quality Assurance Specialists (GS-1910) perform, administer, or advise work to assure the quality of products acquired and used by the Federal Government. The work involves: developing plans and programs for achieving and maintaining product quality throughout the item's life cycle, monitoring operations to prevent the production of defects and to verify adherence to quality plans and requirements, and analyzing and investigating adverse quality trends or conditions and initiation of corrective action.

AGRICULTURAL COMMODITY GRADERS

Agricultural Commodity Graders (GS-1980) administer, supervise, or perform work to examine and evaluate agricultural products based on official standards and related regulations. They determine the official U.S. grades and acceptability of agricultural products in terms of quality or condition. The work often includes inspecting or monitoring the conditions under which the product is: processed, stored, or transported to ensure product quality.

AGRICULTURAL COMMODITY AIDS

Agricultural Commodity Aids (GS-1981) supervise or perform clerical work. In accordance with prescribed standards and regulations, they take samples, make tests, or otherwise assist in the grading or classing of agricultural commodities.

SUPPLY SPECIALISTS

Supply Specialists (GS-2001) perform work of such a general or specific nature that it is not included in any other category. The work generally includes the distribution and storage of supplies.

SUPPLY PROGRAM MANAGERS

Supply Program Managers (GS-2003) manage or provide support work that contributes to the overall management of a supply program which encompasses two or more technical supply activities. They may perform several different types of work, including: managing, directing, or administering supply programs that involve two or more technical supply functions, developing, promoting, and analyzing the policies and methods used to manage supply programs.

SUPPLY CLERKS & TECHNICIANS

Supply Clerks and Technicians (GS-2005) supervise or perform clerical and technical support work. They ensure the effective operation of supply management programs.

INVENTORY MGT SPECIALISTS

Inventory Management Specialists (GS-2010) perform technical work to: manage, regulate, coordinate, plan, determine provisions and requirements, buy and distribute, dispose of supplies, equipment, or other materials.

DISTRIBUTION FACILITY & STORAGE MANAGER

Distribution Facility and Storage Managers (GS-2030) have management responsibility for distribution and storage programs. They perform technical or managerial work to: receive, handle, store, maintain while in storage, issue, or physically control items within a distribution system.

PACKAGING SPECIALISTS

Packaging Specialists (GS-2032) plan, design, and develop packages to protect supplies, materials, and equipment between the time of purchase and use. The packages must prevent environmental and mechanical damage during handling, shipping, and storage. More specifically, the packaging specialist may: determine the best method of packaging particular materials, establish packaging standards, develop or review packaging specifications, evaluate packaging methods, and supervise and manage packaging programs.

SUPPLY CATALOGERS

Supply Catalogers (GS-2050) perform technical work to develop, maintain, or revise supply catalogs, manuals, stock lists, computer input data, item descriptions, and other documents which identify items of supply.

SALES STORE CLERKS

Sales Store Clerks (GS-2091) deal with the retail sale of merchandise or stock items. They supervise or perform: checkouts, sales clerk, customer assistance, or other clerical duties. The work requires the application of clerical knowledge, procedures, and/or practices that are peculiar to sales store operations.

TRANSPORTATION SPECIALSTS

Transportation Specialists (GS-2101) advise, supervise, or perform work which involves two or more specialized transportation functions or other transportation work not specifically included in other categories.

TRANSPORTATION CLERKS & ASSISTANTS

Transportation Clerks and Assistants (GS-2102) perform clerical or technical support work in the field of transportation. The work requires the ability to apply the established: instructions, rules, regulations, and procedures of a transportation or traffic management program.

TRANSPORTATION INDUSTRY ANALYSTS

Transportation Industry Analysts (GS-2110) perform analytical, evaluative, advisory, or similar work to regulate the transportation industry. This includes dealing with: economics, equity in industry practices, and protection of the public interest.

RAILROAD SAFETY INSPECTORS

Railroad Safety Inspectors (GS-2121): develop, administer, or enforce railroad safety standards and regulations, or investigate railroad accidents and attempt to prevent them. These positions require knowledge of: railroad operating practices and record-keeping, the methods used to install, maintain, or manufacture railroad equipment, signal systems, and track, safety practices applicable to the railroad industry and related laws, regulations, and standards, and the investigative techniques used in determining the cause of accidents.

MOTOR CARRIER SAFETY SPECIALIST

Motor Carrier Safety Specialists (GS-2123) ensure the safe operation of commercial motor vehicles on the public highways. They administer, supervise, or perform work to promote or enforce compliance with Federal laws, standards, and regulations.

HIGHWAY SAFETY SPECIALISTS

Highway Safety Specialists (GS-2125): develop and administer highway safety regulations, standards and programs, elicit and promote support for highway safety, identify current highway safety problems, evaluate the effectiveness of highway safety programs and methods, or provide State and local governments with technical assistance to: improve vehicle, passenger, or pedestrian safety, and identify, control, or eliminate the factors that contribute to highway accidents.

TRAFFIC MANAGEMENT SPECIALISTS

Traffic Management Specialists (GS-2130) perform work to: develop policies and plans for traffic management programs, plan and direct traffic operations, or obtain economical and efficient transportation of freight, personal property, passengers, or all three, by common transportation carrier services or other means.

FREIGHT RATE SPECIALISTS

Freight Rate Specialists (GS-2131) deal with the domestic and foreign movement of freight to determine the classification and rates of freight, and/or freight routes prior to shipment. They also perform pre- and post-audits of freight bills to determine the propriety of the rates. They administer, supervise, or perform work to procure common carrier and other transportation service by rail, motor, air, water, and miscellaneous means. More specifically, they study and apply published: classification guides, rate tariffs, dockets, agreements, contracts, and related carrier and Federal publications to classify freight and determine appropriate rates and routes.

TRAVEL ASSISTANTS

Travel Assistants (GS-2132) administer, supervise, or perform work to transport people, individually or in groups, within, to, from, and between the United States, its territories and possessions, and foreign countries.

SHIPMENT CLERKS & ASSISTANTS

Shipment Clerks and Assistants (GS-2134) need a practical knowledge of clerical and technical duties involved in shipping or storing freight or personal property by

162

commercial or Government means. They: arrange for shipment of goods, parcels, or printed materials, determine extent of personal property shipment and storage entitlements at Government expense, arrange for storage, pickup, delivery, and other ancillary services required for shipments, prepare and process shipment and/or storage documents, records, receipts, manifests, etc., for shipping and receiving points, maintain and update vital shipment and storage records or record control systems, and/or coordinate shipment scheduling, expediting, delaying, or other disposition.

TRANSPORTATION LOSS/DAMAGE CLAIMS EXAMINERS

Transportation Loss Damage Claims Examiners (GS-2135) administer, supervise, or perform work to examine, develop, review, or authorize claims by or against the Government. These claims arise from the loss or damage of goods and merchandise while they are being transported. They do not determine transportation rates or develop loss and damage prevention measures.

CARGO SCHEDULERS

Cargo Schedulers (GS-2144) supervise or perform work to control or schedule the movement of cargo into, out of, or through one or more terminals. They determine the proper amounts and time sequences for cargo movement based on: the priority of the cargo, the terminals' ability to accommodate the cargo, and/or the carriers' ability to move the cargo.

TRANSPORTATION OPERATORS

Transportation Operators Specialists (GS-2150) administer, supervise, or perform work to plan, direct, or operate: rail, motor, air, or water transportation systems and service. They may be responsible for operating both transportation and service and terminal facilities.

DISPATCHERS

Dispatchers (GS-2151) supervise or perform clerical work to dispatch or schedule motor vehicles, trains, aircraft, or vessels to transport passengers, mail, equipment, or supplies.

AIR TRAFFIC CONTROLLERS

Air Traffic Controllers (GS-2152) may: Control air traffic to insure safe, orderly and expeditious movement along air routes and at airports. This requires: a knowledge of aircraft separation standards and control techniques, and the ability to apply them properly under conditions of great stress. Provide pre-flight and in-flight assistance to aircraft. This requires: knowledge of the information pilots need to conduct safe flights, and the ability to present that information clearly and concisely.

AIR TRAFFIC ASSISTANTS

Air Traffic Assistants (GS-2154) perform work in support of air traffic control functions. The work requires knowledge of air traffic control procedures. It does not require knowledge of aircraft separation standards or the ability to provide pre-flight or in-flight safety or weather briefings.

MARINE CARGO SPECIALISTS

Marine Cargo Specialists (GS-2161) supervise, administer, monitor, or perform work to plan and/or direct: the loading and stowage of cargo aboard vessels, and the unloading of cargo from vessels.

AIRCRAFT OPERATORS

Aircraft Operators (GS-2181) perform duties such as: piloting or co-piloting aircraft to carry out various programs and functions of Federal agencies, providing ground and flight instruction and in-flight evaluation in the piloting of aircraft, flight testing developmental and modified aircraft and Components, performing in-flight inspection, evaluating air navigation facilities and the environmental conditions affecting instrument flight procedures, performing staff work concerned with planning, analyzing, or administering agency aviation programs, which requires applying pilot knowledge and skills.

AIR NAVIGATORS

Air navigators (GS-2183) assist pilots in aircraft operations by determining, planning, and performing the navigational aspects of the flight. Positions require knowledge of the various methods of air navigation, and skill in using navigational instruments, equipment, and systems in conjunction with flight instruments to direct the movement and positioning of the aircraft to accomplish a specific mission or assignment.

AIRCREW TECHNICIANS

Aircrew Technicians (GS-2185) perform, instruct, or supervise flight crew work, particularly:

(1)   flight engineering work supporting the operation of heavy multiengine aircraft,
(2)   controlling and operating aerial refueling systems aboard tanker aircraft, and
(3)   loading, positioning, and securing cargo in transport aircraft.

APPENDIX 7

JOB FAIRS AND CAREER DAYS CAN MAKE A DIFFERENCE!

If you, or someone you love, are out of work; thinking of changing careers; or just interested in what the trends are with regard to jobs in the United States; you'll want to take advantage of the numerous job fairs and career days being held across the country this year. The Office of Personnel Management was kind enough to share their current list with us -- which we are pleased to pass along to you. As you will notice, some of the job fairs or career days are aimed at specific groups of people, i.e. health care workers, engineers, etc. However, most of them are designed to appeal to everyone. You will want to make special notes on Federal Job Fairs that may be taking place in a location near you. In each instance we have provided a phone number and contact information so that you can obtain additional feedback on specific fairs of interest to you. Good Luck!

ATLANTA REGION JOB FAIRS

MAY 1992:

Meredith College
Teacher
Network Day
Raleigh, NC May 7
Contact: Gordon
Folger
(919) 829-8341

Univer of Central FL
Career Day
Orlando, FL May 7
Contact: Jim Gracey
(407) 823-2361

JULY 1992:

Miami FEB Job Career
Expo, Westside Mall
Miami, FL Date: TBA
Contact: Mark Palazoo
(305) 526-7456

SEPTEMBER 1992:

Mississippi State
Career Day
Mississippi State, MS
September 1-2
Contact: Gloria Reeves
(601) 325-3344

Florida A&M Univ
University,
Career Expo '92
Tallahassee, FL
Sept. 16
Contact: Marti Johnson
(904) 599-3700

Jackson State
Career Day
Jackson, MS Sept. 17
Contact: Obra Hackett
(601) 968-2477

Ringling School of Art
Career Day
Sarasota, FL Sept. 20
Contact: Placement
Director
(813) 351-4614

Florida Atlantic
Univ, Career Day
Boca Raton, FL
September 22
Contact: M. McDonald
(407) 367-3533

OCTOBER 1992:

Tampa College
Career Day
Tampa, FL Date TBA
Contact: C. Tedesco
(813) 879-6000

Tuskegee University
Career Fair
Tuskegee, AL Oct. 1
Contact: Dr. Johnnie
Harris
(205) 727-8294

Alcorn State
Career Fair, Oct. 7
Lorman, MS
Contact: Al Johnson
(601) 877-6324

Samford University
Career Fair
Birmingham, AL
October 7
Contact: Liz Sawyer
(205) 870-2011

University Of Miami
Career Day, Oct. 14
Coral Gables, FL
Contact: Elina Artigas
(305) 284-5451

College of Boca Raton
Career Day, Oct. 21
Boca Raton, FL
Contact: Placement
Director
(407) 944-0770

NOVEMBER 1992:

Webber College
Career Day
Date: TBA
Babson   Park,   FL
Contact: Grady
McClendon
(813) 638-1431

Stetson University
Career Day, Nov. 19
DeLand, FL
Contact: Dawn Rodak
(904) 822-7315

CHICAGO REGION JOB FAIRS

MAY 1992:

Univ of Minnesota
Minneapolis Job Fair
May 5
Contact: Herb
Harmisson
(612) 625-8869

DePaul University
Expd Alumni Job Fair
May 7
Contact: Jane McGrath
(312) 362-8437

Bay de Noo Comm
College, Nursing Job
Fair, May 8, Michigan
Contact: Eileen Hayes
(313) 766-4211

Baker College-Flint
Job Fair, May 8
Flint, MI
Contact: Eileen Hayes
(313) 766-4211

Indiana State Univ
Teacher Recruitment
Fair, May 8
Contact: Robert Elsey
(812) 237-5000

DeVry Institute of
Tech, Career Fair '92
Ohio, May 12
Contact: Denise
Pulgano
(614) 235-7291

JUNE 1992:

De Paul University
Illinois Collegiate Job
Fair, June 9
Contact: Jane McGrath

AUGUST 1992:

DeVry Institute of
Tech. Career Expo III
August 22
Contact: John Petrix
(708) 953-1300

DALLAS REGION JOB FAIRS

SPRING 1992:

Prairie View A&M
Career Day,
Date: TBA
Contact: J.E. Pennywell
(409) 857-2120

Huston-Tillotson
Career Day,
Date: TBA
Austin, TX
Contact: Lavon Marsha
(512) 476-7421

Texas Southern Univ
Career Day Date: TBA
Houston, TX
Contact: Fred Bragg
(713) 527-7225

St. Phillip's College
Career Day
Date: TBA
San Antonio, TX
Contact: Pat Caballero
(512) 531-3397

Univ of Central
Arkansas Career Fair
Date: TBA
Contact: Kathy Rice-
Clayborn
(501) 450-3134

Hendrix College
Career Day
Date: TBA
Conway, AR
Contact: Allison
Nicholas
(501) 450-1372

Arkansas Tech Univ
Career Fair
Date: TBA
Russellville, AR
Contact: Barbara Berry
(501) 968-0278

SEPTEMBER 1992:

Unit of Arkansas, Pine
Bluff Govt Career Info
Day, Sept. 9
Pine Bluff, AR
Contact: Mary Jones
(501) 541-5511

Univ of North Texas
Career Day, Sept. 16
Denton, TX
Contact: Career Svcs
(817) 565-2105

Eastern New Mexico
Univ Career Day
September 16
Portales, MN
Contact: Placement Svc
(505) 562-2211

Northern Arizona Univ
Career Day, Sept. 17
Flagstaff, Az
Contact: Karen
Schrameck
(602) 523-3811

Western NM University
Govt Career Day,
September 21
Contact: Placement
Office
(505) 538-6109

New Mexico State Univ
Govt Career Day
September 22
Engr, Science & Tech
Career Day, Sept. 23
Career Insights, Sept 24
Las Cruces, NM
Contact: Elizabeth
Ortega
(505) 646-1631

Northwestern State
Univ Career Day
Natchitoches, LA
September 22
Contact: Frances
Conine
(318) 357-6011

Univ of Texas, El Paso
Govt Career Day,
September 23
Contact: Brian Carter
(915) 747-5640

Baylor Univ, Career
Day, Sept. 23
Waco, TX
Contact: Mary Beseda
(817) 755-3771

New Mexico Inst of
Mining Career Day
Date: TBA
Albuquerque, NM
Contact: Placement Dir
(505) 286-5389

Southern Univ, Career
Day, Date: TBA
Contact: Ada Green
(504) 286-4686

Dillard Univ Career
Exploration Day
New Orleans
Date: TBA
Contact: Ada Green
(504) 286-4686

Louisiana Tech Univ
Career Day
DATE: TBA
Ruston, LA
Contact: Jan Grigsby
(318) 257-4336

Univ of New Orleans
Govt Career Day
Date: TBA
New Orleans
Contact: Ernestine
Montgomery
(504) 286-6241

Montana State Univ
Career Day Date: TBA
Bozeman, MT
Contact: Career Svcs
(406) 994-4353

Univ of Montana
Career Day Date: TBA
Missoula, MT
Contact: Career Svcs
(406) 243-2022

Colorado State Univ
Career Day Date: TBA
Fort Collins, CO
Contact: Career Svcs
(303) 492-5707

Colorado School of
Mines
Engrs Career Day
Date: TBA
Golden, CO
Contact: Career Svcs
(303) 273-3233

Auraria Campus
Serving Metro State
College of Denver
Career Day Date: TBA
Contact: Career Svcs
(303) 556-3477

Univ of Wyoming
Career Day Date: TBA
Contact: Career Svcs
(303) 766-2309

OCTOBER 1992:

Highlands Univ Career
Day, Oct. 1
Las Vegas, NM
Contact: Career Svcs
(505) 454-3470

Univ of AR at Little
Rock, Govt Career
Opp Day, Oct. 21
Contact: Dianna Kinsey
(501) 569-3185

Univ of S. Colorado
Career Day Date: TBA
Pueblo, CO
Contact: Career Svcs
(719) 549-2581

El Paso Comm College
College Job Fair
Date: TBA
Contact: Career Ctr
(915) 594-2417

Univ of New Mexico
Govt Career Day
Date: TBA
Contact: Career Svcs
(505) 277-2531

Westminster College
Career Day Date: TBA
Salt Lake City, UT
Contact: Career Svcs
(801) 484-7651

Univ of New Mexico
Hispanic Engr
Career Day Date: TBA
Contact: HEO
(505) 277-6610

Bernalillo High School
Annual College Career
Day, Date: TBA
Contact: Charlotte
Case
(505) 867-2388

Dillard Univ Grad &
Professional School
Career Day Date: TBA
New Orleans, LA
Contact: Ada Green
(504) 286-4686

Centenary College
Career Fair
Date: TBA
Shreveport, LA
Contact: Lee Anne
Turner
(318) 869-5042

NOVEMBER 1992:

Albuquerque-Santa Fe
Los Alamos EEO
Highlands Univ
Date: Nov. 3
Las Vegas, NV
Contact: Ethel Chavez
(505) 766-3639

Delgado Community
College Job Fair
November 11
New Orleans, LA
Contact: Nita Hutter
(504) 483-4296

Louisiana State Job
Fair, Location Pending
Date: TBA
Contact: B.J. Francis
(504) 342-3013

Santa Fe Community
College Career Fair
Date: TBA
Contact: Irene Charles
(505) 438-1270

Univ of Utah, Career
Day, Date: TBA
Salt Lake City, UT
Contact: Diana Hirschi
(801) 581-7785

Univ of NM
Valencia Career Day
Date: TBA
Contact: Career Svcs
(505) 865-9667

Southwestern Indian
Polytechnic Institute
Govt Fall Career Day
Date: TBA
Contact: Placement
Office
(505) 897-5325

Regis College, Career
Day, Denver, CO
Date: TBA
Contact: Career Svcs
(303) 458-3508

Mesa State College
Fed Career Fair
Date: TBA
Grand Junction, CO
Contact: Ellen
Trinkline
(303) 242-0731

New Orleans Career
Directions 2000 Job
Fair, Date: TBA
Contact: Alma Jackson
(504) 566-0204

SAN FRANCISCO REGION JOB FAIRS

MAY 1992:

Los Medanos College
Career Fair
Date: TBA
Pittsburg, CA
Contact: Dave
Mendinsky
(415) 439-2181

College of Alameda
Career Fair
Date: TBA
Contact: Joyce Blair
(510) 748-2232

Canada College Career
Fair, Date: TBA
Redwood City, CA
Contact: Joan Delgardo
(415) 306-3209

Cabrillo College
Career Fair
Date: TBA
Watsonville, CA
Contact: Lynn Hood
(408) 479-6540

Hartnell College
Career Fair
Date: TBA
Salinas, CA
Contact: Ruth
McMullen
(408) 755-6925

Monterey Peninsula
College Career Fair
Date: TBA
Contact: Terry
Advincula
(408) 646-4010

Napa Valley College
Career Fair
Date: TBA
Contact: Deborah
Finley
(707) 253-3055

City College of San
Francisco Job Fair
Date: TBA
Contact: Josephine
Ubungen
(415) 239-3117

Ohione College
Minority Job Fair
Date: TBA
Fremont, CA
Contact: Gail Marx
(510) 659-6128

Sonoma State Univ
Career America Week
May 5, Rohnert Park
Contact: Ron Logsdon
(707) 664-2196

Cal State Fresno
Career Fair, May 6
Contact: Caroline
Williams
(209 294-2381

College of the Sequoias
Career Fair, May 6
Visalia, CA
Contact: Floyd Hord
(209) 730-3730

Umpqua Comm
College College,
Career Day, May 6
Roseburg, OR
Contact: Sue Windosr
(503) 440-4600

San Jose State Univ
Last Chance Job Fair
May 14
Contact: Margaret
Wilkes
(408) 924-6010

Yakima Valley Comm
College Career Day
May 14
Contact: Linda Radford
(509) 575-2363

FALL 1992:

Univ of Alaska
Fairbanks Career Day
October 14
Contact: Dennis Long
(907) 474-7596

Univ of Hawaii Govt
Career Day
Sept or Oct
Contact: Irene Lee
(808) 956-8605

Family Support &
Career Fair Oct or Nov
Elmendorf AFB, AK
Contact: Pam Pardy
(907) 552-4943

**METROPOLITAN
WASHINGTON D.C.
JOB FAIRS:**

Job Fairs for People
With Disabilities
May 18-19
Contact: Margaret
Johnson
(202) 606-2686

Clerical, Secretarial &
Administrative Job Fair
June 1992, Date: TBA
Contact: Joe Ruiz
(202) 606-2701

Health, Science &
Technology Job Fair
Washington DC Conv
Center, August 20-21
Contact: Margaret
Johnson
(202) 606-2686

WINTER 1992:

Health, Science &
Technology Job Fair
Date & Location TBA
Contact: Margaret
Johnson
(202) 606-2686

**PHILADELPHIA
REGION JOB FAIRS:**

Office of Pers Mgmt.
Career Day, April 2
Contact: Terry Reed-
Evans
(215) 597-7163

APPENDIX 8

Sometimes when you're looking for government work, you have to keep your eyes and ears open for one-of-a-kind opportunities, or out of the usual procedures. The following are some bits of information that may assist you.

DOES PROTECTING THE ENVIRONMENT INTEREST YOU?

The Environmental Protection Agency has a national hotline number to recruit new employees. This EPA National Recruitment Program Number enables potential hirees to contact the agency for employment information and assists EPA managers in locating and hiring qualified employees to fill vacant positions. If you are interested in serving not only your country -- but humanity -- a career with EPA may be right up your alley The hotline operates between 8:30 a.m. and 4:30 p.m. Monday through Friday (EST):

EPA HOTLINE: 1 (800) 338-1350

WONDERING IF YOU CAN QUALIFY FOR A GOVERNMENT JOB?

There's an office in Washington, D.C., which handles the standards for evaluating employment requirements for most government occupations. They set the minimum qualification standards for each of the agencies hiring. If you would like to find our more information on the particular qualifications for a job you're interested in, contact:

Office of Classifications
Qualification Standards Branch
Career Entry and Employee Dev. Group
Office of Personnel Management
199 E. St., NW Room 6515
Washington, DC 20415
(202) 632-0557

If you're having trouble choosing a career, trying to change jobs, or finding a job, the federal government has plenty of help available at very little or not cost. Not only will you be able to find out where the job opportunities are, you will also be able to get official estimates of what the job market will be for ANY profession next year, or even five years from now. If you need to know what part of the country is best for teachers, paralegals, engineers, etc. -- you can usually find out in just one phone call. Perhaps you're trying to choose a college major that will assure you a

173

good chance of find work when you graduate -- this sort of information is also available. Besides help finding a job, you can also find job training and retraining vocational programs. There is also assistance for special groups such as the disabled, women re-entering the job market, veterans, and for those of you who have been laid off from work.

YOUTH - 2000

Youth 2000 is a nationwide call to action between now and the year 2000. This program is designed to enlist the involvement of all sectors of society to help youth at risk achieve social and economic self-sufficiency and fulfill their potential to become contribution members of society. Youth 200 brings the Departments of Labor and Health and Human Services together to focus the energies of state and local government, on opportunities and challenges facing our nation and its youth. Employment and Training Administration regional offices worth with state and community leaders each year to promote public awareness of youth related issues and also continues efforts to stimulate new discussion, which is an important step in arousing the wherewithal to address issues associated with at-risk youth. These avenues include battling illiteracy, high school drop outs, teen pregnancy, and alcohol and drug use. If you would like more information on programs that are available in your area, please contact:

> At-Risk Youth
> Employment Information Office, ETA
> U.S. Department of Labor
> 200 Constitution Ave., NW, Room S2322
> Washington, DC 20210
> (202) 523-6871

CAREER ENCYCLOPEDIA AND PROSPECTS

The Occupational Outlook Handbook is an encyclopedia of careers which covers 225 occupations. For each of these there is information on what the work is like, employment figures, educational and training requirements, advancement possibilities, job prospects through the year 2000, earnings-related occupations, and where you can obtain more information. The handbooks costs $22.00. The Occupational Outlook Quarterly can help students stay in touch with current occupational and employment developments between editions of the handbook. The Quarterly supplement provides readers with advice on how to get a job, articles on new occupations, plus addresses and phone numbers to assist in getting more information on apprenticeships and training. It also provides scholarship information. The Quarterly costs $5.00 a year. Both of these books are available at your public library, or if you wish a personal copy you can contact:

Career Encyclopedia and Prospects
Office of Information
Bureau of Labor Statistics
U.S. Department of Labor
441 G Street, NW
Washington, DC 20212
(202) 523-1221
                    or
Superintendent of Documents
Government Printing Office
Washington, DC 20402
(202) 783-3238

DISPLACED HOMEMAKERS

The Displaced Homemakers Network is the only national organization which addresses the specific concerns of women who are being forced into a job market for which have had little preparation. This program is supported by the Women's Bureau of the U.S. Department of Labor. Through its Washington, D.C. office, this organization works to increase displaced homemakers options for economic self-sufficiency, provides information about the public policy issues which affect displaced homemakers, and provides technical assistance for service providers. Additionally they help programs that work for displaced homemakers. There are numbers publications and newsletters available, and the staff can assist you in locating a displaced homemakers program near you. For more information contact:

Displaced Homemakers Job Network
1411 K Street, NW
Suite 930
Washington, DC 20005
(202) 467-6346

DISABLED VETERANS

Most employment service offices provide a Disabled Veterans Outreach Program which is staffed by veterans who provide special assistance to other vets and help them obtain employment and training services. The DVOP staff develops networks of employer contacts and work with community groups and veterans

175

organizations in an effort to locate jobs for their clients. This program is aimed only at disabled and Vietnam-era veterans. If you have checked with your local employment service office and cannot find this service available, simply contact:

Disabled Veterans/Job Matching Service
Veterans Employment and Training
U.S. Department of Labor
200 Constitution Ave., NW, Room S1313
Washington, DC 20210
(202) 523-9110

EXPERIMENTAL JOB TRAINING OPPORTUNITIES

The office of Strategic Planning and Policy Development at the U.S. Department of Labor plans and implements Pilot and Demonstration Programs to provide job training, employment opportunities, and related services for individuals which specific disadvantages. These programs address industry-wide skill shortages and offer technical expertise to particular client groups. Additionally, they develop information networks among organizations with similar Job Training Partnership Act related objectives. These programs are administered at the national level and then operated at the state and local level. The programs cover disadvantaged groups in the labor market as follows: offenders, individuals with limited English language skills, handicapped persons, women, single parents, displaced homemakers, youth, older works, those who lack education credentials, and public assistance recipients. For more information on the types of programs currently available contact:

Experimental Job Training Opportunities
Office of Strategic Planning and Policy Development
Employment and Training Administration
U.S. Department of Labor
200 Constitution Ave., NW, Room N5637
Washington, DC 20210
(202) 535-0677

THERE'S SOMETHING FISHY GOING ON HERE

If you love the great outdoors, this may be for you! The National Fisheries Center and its five field stations are world-renowned as a focal point for fish health research and for the development of fisheries. Students who attend the academy study nutrition, genetics, diseases, management technology and technical services. If you're interested in a career in fish husbandry, you'll want to contact:

Fish Husbandry Training Academy
National Fisheries Center
U.S. Fish and Wildlife Service
Box 700
Kearneysville, WV 25430
(304) 725-8461, Ext. 5333

APPRENTICESHIP LIVES!!!

Apprenticeship is a combination of on-the-job training and related classroom instruction in which workers learn the practical and theoretical aspects of a highly skilled occupation. Apprenticeship programs are operated on a voluntary basis by employers, employer associations, or management and labor groups, The role of the federal government is to encourage and promote the establishment of apprenticeship programs and provide technical assistance to program sponsors. The related classroom instruction is given int he program sponsor's training facility or a local technical school or junior college. For more information about programs that may be available in your area contact:

Bureau of Apprenticeship and Training
Employment and Training Administration
U.S. Department of Labor
200 Constitution Ave., NW, Room N4649
Washington, DC 20210
(202) 523-0540

THE JOB CORPS CAN CHANGE YOUR LIFE

The Job Corps is a federally administered national employment and training program designed to serve severely disadvantaged you ages 16 to 21. Enrollees are provided with food, housing, education, vocational training, medical care, counseling and other support services. The program is designed to prepare youth for stable, productive employment and the ability to enter into vocational/technical schools or other institutions for further education or training. Job Crops centers range in capacity from 175 to 2,600 enrollees. Some of the centers are operated by the U.S. Departments of Interior and Agriculture (civilian conservation centers), with the remaining centers operating under contracts with the U.S. Department of Labor primarily by major corporations. Vocational training is given in such occupations as auto repair, carpentry, painting, nursing, business and clerical skills, as well as preparation for the GED high school equivalency exam. If you are interested in an application contact:

Office of Job Crops
Employment and Training Administration
U.S. Department of Labor
200 Constitution Ave., NW, Room N4510
Washington, DC 20210
(202) 535-0550
Alumni Association Toll Free:
(800) 424-2866

THE SENIOR COMMUNITY SERVICE EMPLOYMENT PROGRAM

The Senior Community Service Employment Program is sponsored by state and territorial governments and eight national organizations to promote the creation of part-time jobs in community service activities for jobless, low-income persons who are at least 55 years of age and have poor prospects of employment. Individuals are hired to work part-time at senior citizens centers, in schools or hospitals, in programs for the handicapped, in fire prevention programs and on beautification and restoration projects. This program makes possible an array of community services for the elderly. Participants must be at least 55 years of age, have family income of not more than 25% above the federal poverty level, and be capable of performing the tasks to which they are assigned. Your local job service office should be able to provide you with more detailed information. You may also get data from your state or area office for the aging or contact:

Office of Special Targeted Programs
Employment and Training Administration
U.S. Department of Labor
200 Constitution Ave., NW, Room N4643
Washington, DC 20210
(202) 535-0157

MATCHING YOURSELF WITH THE WORKWORLD

The Government printing office offers a booklet designed to assist you in comparing job characteristics with your own skills and interests. The publication is called Matching Yourself With World of Work and contains 17 occupational characteristics and requirements, then matches your characteristics with 200 occupations chosen from the Occupational Outlook Handbook. This book can be ordered for $1.00:

Government Printing Office
Washington, DC 20402
(202) 783-3238

OCCUPATIONAL EXPLORATION ENCYCLOPEDIA

The Guide For Occupational Exploration is an invaluable reference source which provides detailed occupational and labor market information you can use to find and keep a job. The Guide groups thousands of occupations by the interests, traits and abilities required for successful performance. Additionally it provides descriptions of each work group and assists individuals in reviewing, understanding and evaluating their own interests so they can transfer these into a work environment. You may be able to find this publication in your public library. There is also a workbook to be used with this text. If you are unable to locate this book at the library contact:

Superintendent of Documents
Government Printing Office
Washington, DC 20402
(202) 783-3238

HOW IS OFFICE AUTOMATION AFFECTING WOMEN'S JOBS?

The Women's Bureau of the U.S. Department of Labor is highly interested in the impact of automation on the quality of worklife -- as well as on the economic well-being -- of clerical workers and their families. They offer a free publication called Women and Office Automation: Issues for the Decade Ahead. This booklet discusses the quality of work, training and retraining, homebased clerical work, and health and safety issues. If you would like a copy simply contact:

Women's Bureau
U.S. Department of Labor
200 Constitution Ave., NW, Room N4703
Washington, DC 20210
(202) 535-0577

MORE ASSISTANCE FOR LAID OFF WORKERS

If you become totally or partially separated from employment because of increased import competition, the Trade Act of 1974 may provide assistance to you. Such assistance may consist of training, job search and relocation allowances, special help in finding a new job, and weekly cash benefits equal to the level of regular unemployment compensation payable in your state (you must exhaust all unemployment insurance benefits available in your state before collecting weekly cash benefits under the Trade Act.) If you would like more information on this program contact:

Office of Trade Adjustment Assistance
Employment and Training Administration
U.S. Department of Labor
601 D St., NW, Room 6434
Washington, DC 20210
(202) 523-0555

GET OFF WELFARE WITH JOB TRAINING PROVIDED BY OUR GOVERNMENT!

Under the Work Incentive program, employment, training and social supportive services such as child care, housing assistance, medical services, etc., are available to public welfare applicants and recipients in order to enable them to become self-supporting and independent of welfare assistance. All welfare applicants and recipients need to register with the WIN program. If you, or someone you know would like more information contact:

Employment and Training Administration
U.S. Department of Labor
200 Constitution Ave., NW, Room N4470
Washington, DC 20210
(202) 523-0555/Ron Putz

YOUTH CONSERVATION CORPS - YOUR KIDS CAN CHANGE THEIR FUTURE!

If you have a child between the ages of 15 through 18 looking for summer work, you might suggest they think about the Park Service's Youth Conservation Corps. The Corps offers summer employment where workers perform conservation work on public lands. The program is also administered by the Forest Service of the U.S. Department of Agriculture. Work includes constructing trails, building campground facilities, planting trees collecting litter, clearing streams, improving wildlife habitats, and office work. Positions are limited so you will want to contact:

U.S. Youth Conservation Corps
U.S. Fish and Wildlife Service
National Park Service
Washington, DC 20240
(202) 343-5514

NOTES

NOTES

NOTES

NOTES

NOTES

NOTES